Prayer Steps to Serenity
Daily Quiet Time Edition

Books by L.G. Parkhurst, Jr.

Prayer Steps to Serenity: The Twelve Steps Journey
New Serenity Prayer Edition
Edmond: Agion Press, 2006

How God Teaches Us to Pray:
Lessons from the Lives of Francis and Edith Schaeffer
Milton Keynes, England: Nelson Word Ltd. 1993.

How to Pray in the Spirit
Compiled and edited from the works of John Bunyan
Grand Rapids: Kregel Publications, 1993, 1998.

Principles of Prayer
Compiled and edited from the works of Charles Finney
Minneapolis: Bethany House Publishers, 1980, 2001.

Answers to Prayer
Compiled and edited from the works of Charles Finney
Minneapolis: Bethany House Publishers, 1983, 2002.

Principles of Devotion
Compiled and edited from the works of Charles Finney
Minneapolis: Bethany House Publishers, 1987.

Principles of Union with Christ
Compiled and edited from the works of Charles Finney
Minneapolis: Bethany House Publishers, 1985.

Principles of Righteousness: Finney's Lessons on Romans, Volume I
Compiled and edited from the works of Charles Finney
Edmond: Agion Press, 2006.

Prayer Steps to Serenity
Daily Quiet Time Edition

L. G. Parkhurst, Jr.

AGION PRESS
P.O. Box 1052
Edmond, Oklahoma 73083-1052
AgionPress.com

Prayer Steps to Serenity
Daily Quiet Time Edition

Copyright © 2006 Louis Gifford Parkhurst, Jr. All Rights Reserved.

No part of this book may be reproduced or transmitted in any form or by any means, graphic, electronic, or mechanical, including photocopying, recording, taping, or by any information storage retrieval system, without the prior written permission of the copyright owners.

Unless otherwise noted, all Scripture quotations in this book are from the *Holy Bible: New International Version*, copyright 1973, 1978, 1984, by the International Bible Society. Used by permission of Zondervan Bible Publishers.

Prayer Steps to Serenity: Daily Quiet Time Edition is abridged and extensively revised from *Prayer Steps to Serenity: The Twelve Steps Journey, New Serenity Prayer Edition*: Edmond: Agion Press © 2006 Louis Gifford Parkhurst, Jr. The *Daily Quiet Time Edition* is an alternate edition for those not interested in working the 12 Steps as presented in most recovery programs. Visit the *Prayer Steps to Serenity* website at PrayerSteps.org for more information.

Cover Photo Copyright © 2000 Andrew Hedges. Used by Permission.
Cover Design and Graphics Copyright © 2004, 2005 by Kathryn Winterscheidt. Used by Permission.

ISBN: 978-0-9778053-7-2 (pbk) *Prayer Steps to Serenity: Daily Quiet Time Edition*

ISBN: 978-0-9778053-8-9 (pbk) *Prayer Steps to Serenity: The Twelve Steps Journey: New Serenity Prayer Edition*

Contents

Preface 9

Step 1—Discover Your Needs
1 The Source of All My Power—*John 15:5* 11
2 The Good Fight of Faith—*1 Timothy 6:12* 13
3 The Right Attitude in Prayer—*2 Timothy 4:7* 15
4 God Meets Me in My Defects—*Ephesians 3:20, 21* 17
5 God's Power Can Fill My Emptiness—*Ephesians 1:19, 20* 19

Step 2—Reach Beyond Yourself
6 A Cure for My Anxiety—*Philippians 4:6* 21
7 Overcoming My Greatest Stumbling Block—*Matthew 11:28* ... 23
8 Jesus Makes Me New—*2 Corinthians 5:17* 25
9 My Power from on High—*Luke 24:49* 27
10 The Secret of My Power in Prayer—*John 14:15, 16* 29

Step 3—Trust in God
11 Taking Time with God—*Ecclesiastes 3:1* 31
12 Willing God's Will—*Matthew 26:39* 33
13 From My Strength to God's—*Psalm 84:5, 7* 35
14 The Spirit Will Pray for Me—*Romans 8:26*.................. 37
15 Thanking God for His Care—*Zechariah 12:10*................ 39

Step 4—Examine Your Life
16 The Root Cause of My Problems—*1 John 1:8*................ 41
17 God Reveals My Problems the Best—*1 John 1:7*............ 43
18 The Problem of Prayerlessness—*1 Samuel 12:23*............ 45
19 The One Who Can Save Me—*Matthew 1:21* 47
20 My Reason for Rejoicing—*Luke 23:34*....................... 49

Step 5—Admit Your Mistakes
21 Conscience and Confession—*1 John 1:9* 51
22 Life Follows Death to Self—*John 12:24*..................... 53
23 God's Forgiveness Inspires My Love—*Exodus 34:6, 7* 55
24 God Will Forgive My Prayerlessness—*Matthew 6:6*........... 57
25 My Forgiveness Brings Singing—*Psalm 32:5*................. 59

Step 6—Transform Your Thinking
26 God Will Remove My Fear—*Luke 1:74, 75*................... 61
27 Jesus Promises to Transform Me—*John 14:1, 14*............. 63
28 I Can Become More Like God—*Leviticus 11:44* 65
29 Receiving the Fullness of God—*Philippians 2:5* 67
30 Prayer Leads Me to Victory—*Romans 7:24, 25*............... 69

Step 7—Remove Your Defects
31 God's Wonderful Promises to Me—*Hebrews 8:12* 71
32 God Will Work Wonders in Me—*Ephesians 3:16, 17*.......... 73
33 God's Love Will Remove My Hatred—*John 15:12*............. 75
34 My Whole Life Depends on Jesus—*John 14:1*................ 77
35 I Know God Will Help Me—*Hebrews 11:1*................... 79

Step 8—Think of Others

36 Some Benefits of Making Amends—*John 13:34* 81
37 Forgiving Helps Me Make Amends—*Mark 11:25* 83
38 I Will Take Up My Cross—*Matthew 10:38, 30*. 85
39 Willing to Give Up Everything—*Luke 14:33* 87
40 Willing to Face What I Lack—*Mark 10:21* 89

Step 9—Right Your Wrongs

41 I Will Avoid Making Excuses—*Philippians 2:14, 15* 91
42 The Holy Spirit Will Help Me—*John 16:14* 93
43 When Christ Is My Life—*Colossians 3:4* 95
44 Prayer Helps in Making Amends—*Ephesians 6:18*............. 97
45 I Will Not Give Up—*Luke 18:1* 99

Step 10—Practice Doing Right

46 Reasons for Lack of Prayer—*Romans 12:3*. 101
47 Overcoming Satan—*Ephesians 6:12* 103
48 I Train with a Goal—*1 Corinthians 9:26, 27*. 105
49 Abiding in Christ—*2 Corinthians 4:10, 12* 107
50 I Died on Christ's Cross—*1 Peter 2:24*....................... 109

Step 11—Pray to God

51 True Prayer Leads to True Fellowship—*Colossians 1:27* 111
52 God Will Not Forsake Me—*Psalm 9:10* 113
53 I Am Crucified to Overcome—*Galatians 2:20*............... 115
54 Reasons for Effective Prayer—*James 5:16*. 117
55 Reasons for Daily Prayer—*Luke 11:3* 119

Step 12—Seek to Serve

56 The Power of Intercession—*2 Corinthians 5:20* 121
57 God Calls Me to Tell Others—*Acts 1:8* 123
58 What May Set Me Apart—*John 15:26, 27*.................... 125
59 My Personal Testimony—*Acts 4:31, 32*...................... 127
60 My Future Work Carrying the Message—*Matthew 4:9*........ 129

Thoughts on Prayer

"You will keep him in perfect peace, whose mind is stayed on you: because he trusts in you."
Isaiah 26:3 in the *King James Version*

"The Holy Spirit prays for us by inspiring our minds. Not that He immediately suggests to us words, or guides our language, but He enlightens our minds and makes the truth take hold of our souls. He leads us to a deep consideration of the state of things, and the result of this is deep inspiration and yearning."
Charles G. Finney in *Principles of Prayer*

"True prayer is a sincere, sensible, affectionate pouring out of the heart or soul to God, through Christ, in the strength and assistance of the Holy Spirit, for such things as God has promised, or according to the Word of God, for the good of the Church, with submission in faith to the will of God."
John Bunyan in *How to Pray in the Spirit*

Preface

The daily meditations in *Prayer Steps to Serenity: Daily Quiet Time Edition* will help you enjoy each day with a peaceful spirit, so you can bring positive changes into your life. The sixty short meditations can by read in sixty days. On the other hand, you may prefer to read one meditation in the morning and another in the evening. Read the meditations in the order in which they appear, for they do follow a progressive and logical plan to help you grow mentally and spiritually. I encourage you to read this book everyday, and then quietly think about the teachings in that day's reading. Through daily prayer steps, God will enable you to:

> ➢ Quiet your mind and emotions to enjoy inner peace

> ➢ Think about your real needs and how to meet them

> ➢ Manage your life in ways that will lead to lasting happiness

> ➢ Talk to God and others easily, effectively and enjoyably

> ➢ Mend broken relationships and restore shattered dreams

> Dream new dreams and achieve new purposes

Practicing a daily "Quiet Time" will enable you to spend more time alone with God. At the end of each reading, spend some time with God in prayer. Listen to God as He speaks to you through His word. Talk to God about your needs and problems. Ask God to show you His will for your life. Commit your day and plans to God. Ask God to give you His power for that day.

More specifically, these suggestions will help you make the most of your "Quiet Time." Read the Scripture—then pause. Close your eyes. Ask God to tell you what He wants you to learn from His word. God will probably not speak to you directly and audibly. However, ask yourself, "What does this scripture reading mean to me?" God will help you think through the meaning and apply it to your life. After you have read the scripture and prayed, read the meditation. After you read the meditation, take a few quiet moments to ask yourself, "What is God saying to me in this meditation?" Read the scripture verse again and seek the answer. Ask, "What is the most important idea I have learned from this reading today?" Think about how you can make your day better by applying what you have learned from prayer and reading. Write your prayers or answer the questions or record your thoughts in the white space below each reading. Close the book. Quietly talk to God about those things you think are most important for your life and for the day ahead. If you read your meditation in the evening, ask God to show you what He wants you to do the next day. Pray for God to give you the courage, wisdom and power to do what He says according to His word. Talk to God in your own words, trusting the Holy Spirit to lead you in prayer. Take time to write down your requests to God; then write down His answers so you can know when God answers you and you can thank God for the answers.

Prayer Steps to Serenity: Daily Quiet Time Edition includes many of the foundational biblical and spiritual principles published in *Prayer Steps to Serenity: The Twelve Steps Journey: New Serenity Prayer Edition*. The *Daily Quiet Time Edition* omits the prayers, the Serenity Prayer meditations, the Twelve Steps Recovery Program, and the personal and group Journey Guides that make *Prayer Steps to Serenity: The Twelve Steps Journey* a helpful book of daily readings and workbook for those working the Twelve Steps to overcome addictions, compulsions or others weaknesses. If you enjoy the devotional readings in the *Daily Quiet Time Edition*, recommend *Prayer Steps to Serenity: The Twelve Steps Journey* to those working (or needing to work) any 12 Steps Program. The *Daily Quiet Time Edition* may introduce someone in denial to the 12 Steps in a non-threatening format or be used for a Bible Study in your home or church.

Discover Your Needs

1

The Source of All My Power

I am the vine; you are the branches. If a man remains in me and I in him, he will bear much fruit; apart from me you can do nothing.

—John 15:5

Because of pride, we can proudly begin to think that we are making ourselves better and do not need anyone else. Yet, apart from God, we are powerless. Without God, we do not have the power to do anything good, either for others or ourselves. Without God, our weaknesses will always defeat us. In fact, apart from God, we only fight against God, others, and even ourselves. Without God's help, we are unwilling to make the necessary and needed changes in our lives.

Jesus truly offers to change our lives and bless us when He promises, "apart from me you can do nothing." We need to remember that apart from Jesus, we cannot even pray or go to God for help. Apart from Jesus, we are not able to discern God's purposes or receive the power to achieve God's will for our lives.

Today, I have many good reasons to give thanks. For one, Jesus promises that when I come to Him, for Him to direct my life, He will unite himself with me. He will dwell within me and never leave me. I need to admit that I cannot manage every area of my life perfectly. In some areas, I just feel powerless to do the right thing, even when I know the right thing to do. When I ask Jesus to give me power to change so I can bless others, He will. Through daily prayer, meditation on the scriptures, and obedience, I can open my life to Him. Then, He will be able to live in me, to work in me, and to work through me each day—all day long. I may be powerless all by myself, but God's power will work in me and through me.

I can have good reason for continuous joy and encouragement—the Lord Jesus can work in me! I need to remind myself daily that without God I am powerless. I need to depend on Him to care for me, and work through me all the day, one day at a time—sometimes moment-by-moment. Whenever I recall, "apart from Me, you can do nothing," I need to remember Jesus' other promise, "The one who abides in Me bears much fruit." I want to start bearing much good fruit to bless the lives of others, especially those whose lives I have been hurting through my selfish or self-centered behavior. I will abide in Christ, and share His love with others. In Christ, I will bear much good fruit. I will believe His promises today.

*Today's Date:*_____

Today's Requests:

Answers to Prayer and Thanksgivings:

Discover Your Needs

2

The Good Fight of Faith

Fight the good fight of the faith. Take hold of the eternal life to which you were called when you made your good confession in the presence of many witnesses.

—1 Timothy 6:12

When I try to pray in my own strength, I am always disappointed and discouraged. However, I have found a struggle that leads to victory. The Bible speaks of it as "the good fight of faith." This fight springs from within me, and I can carry it on by faith. When I get the right understanding of faith, I can stand unmoved in faith.

Jesus is the Author and Finisher of my faith. The Bible teaches: "Let us fix our eyes on Jesus, the Author and Finisher of our faith, who for the joy set before him endured the cross, scorning its shame, and sat down at the right hand of the throne of God" (Hebrews 12:2). When I enter into a right relationship with Jesus, He assures me of His help and power in prayer each moment of every day. The work that He has begun in me He will bring to completion for He is also the Author and Finisher of my faith in Him.

To receive God's help, I first need to say in my heart, "I cannot strive in my own strength and succeed. I need to cast myself at the feet of the Lord Jesus. I will wait on Him in the certain confidence that He will be with me and will work in me. I know that He can help me overcome all my temptations and weaknesses with His power."

Secondly, I need to commit myself to Him and say, "I will strive in prayer. I will let faith fill my heart. Through faith, I will be strong in the Lord, and in the power of His might."

Thirdly, I need to remind myself always that I do not need to fight this fight alone. I have discovered what many have learned by experience: "I labor, struggling with all His energy, which so powerfully works in me" (Colossians 1:29). I struggle to overcome my difficulties. I labor to bless others with my words and actions. Yet, it is the power of Jesus Christ in me that gives me the energy and power I need to overcome all of my obstacles and win the victory in Him.

*Today's Date:*_____

Today's Requests:

Answers to Prayer and Thanksgivings:

Discover Your Needs

3

The Right Attitude in Prayer

> *I have fought the good fight, I have finished the race, I have kept the faith.*
>
> —2 Timothy 4:7

If my heart is cold and dark as I begin to pray, I cannot force myself into a right attitude. All I can do in these times is bow before God and honestly let Him see my real condition. I need to remind Him and myself that He is my only hope. With a childlike trust, I can trust Him to have mercy upon me. I have nothing—He has everything.

I have found that faith in the love of Jesus is the only way I can get into fellowship with God in prayer. I remind myself of His love for me when I recite from memory: "For God so loved the world that he gave his one and only Son, that whoever believes in him shall not perish but have eternal life" (John 3:16). Reading the Bible will open the door for me to hear God's welcome invitation to come into His presence, pray, and have everlasting fellowship with Him. The Holy Spirit will fill me with the love of God when I seek fellowship with Jesus Christ through prayer and reading the scriptures. The Holy Spirit will also give me the wisdom to understand the truth of God in the Bible and guide me in my daily decisions.

I fight two spiritual battles. In the first battle, I must try to conquer my spirit of prayerlessness by ceasing to trust in my own strength. To win this fight, I need to give up my restless efforts and fall helpless at the feet of my loving Lord Jesus. He will speak the word, and my soul will live. He will speak the word to me through the Scriptures I read and remember from heart. He knows my needs and helps me.

Winning the second battle requires me to be deeply earnest. I need to exercise all the power God gives me to overcome my weaknesses. Through searching prayer, I watch over my heart. I pray for God to reveal to me the least moral or spiritual weaknesses in my life. I ask Him to help me overcome any proneness I have to disobey Him whenever I am tempted.

Above all, to have the right attitude in prayer, I need to surrender to God and live a life of personal self-sacrifice. Jesus sacrificed His life for me. I can do no less. If I seek to save my life, I will lose it, but if I lose my life for His sake, I will gain it. God really desires to see this attitude within me. If I surrender to Him, He will work out all things for my good. He will give me the victory over self and selfishness that separates me from Him and others.

*Today's Date:*_____

Today's Requests:

Answers to Prayer and Thanksgivings:

Discover Your Needs

4

God Meets Me in My Defects

Now to him who is able to do immeasurably more than all we ask or imagine, according to his power that is at work within us, to him be glory in the church and in Christ Jesus throughout all generations, for ever and ever! Amen.

—Ephesians 3:20, 21

How prone I am to slide backward in my deliverance from sin! I find it easy to give in to my weaknesses. I limit God's power. I begin to think that God cannot do greater things. I have such limited concepts of God's promises, power, and personality! Too often, when I have failed, I have blamed God and others. When I have been powerless, I have thought God has been helpless. When my life has been out of control, I have accused God of incompetence. When considering my needs, I have sometimes denounced God for being a poor provider.

I need to ask God to make His real nature and character known to me. Each day, I need to admit that I am powerless to overcome my difficulties. To find real help, I need God as God really is. The god of my imagination is not present to help me. God gave us His name: "I Am, Who I Am" or "I Am, Who I Will Be" (Exodus 3:14). The true God is the God we need. As I read the Scriptures, and as I share fellowship with God and other believers, I will learn more about God. The true God loves me, comes to me, saves me, and gives me good success.

I need to know by experience that God is all-powerful. In daily prayer and study of the Bible, I can learn the glorious truth that God is the All-Sufficient One. If I wait on His Spirit, God will open my heart to understand His promises and my real needs. The Comforter will help me see what great things God will give me in answer to prayer.

God really longs to bestow new and better things on those who pray to Him. Can I believe this today? Can I face the truth about myself? Can I face the real nature and character of God, a holy and loving God? Can I admit that I have character defects, but that God has none? Can I admit that I am weak, but God is strong?

I need a deep and soul-searching humility in my prayer life. As my self-confidence decreases, my God-confidence must increase, or I will become more hopeless and weak. God wants me to trust in His omnipotence. He wants me to pray with an increasing and believing boldness. He wants me to express my great need for deliverance in the faith that He will graciously save me from destruction and help me overcome all my weaknesses.

*Today's Date:*_____

Today's Requests:

Answers to Prayer and Thanksgivings:

Discover Your Needs

5

God's Power Can Fill My Emptiness

I pray also that the eyes of your heart may be enlightened in order that you may know the hope to which he has called you, the riches of his glorious inheritance in the saints, and his incomparably great power for us who believe. That power is like the working of his mighty strength.

—Ephesians 1:18, 19

No matter how weak and powerless I feel, I need to remember that the almighty power of God will work within me and never fail me.

God helps me accept the fact that I am powerless to overcome my addictions, dependencies, misbehaviors, temptations, weaknesses, and sins all by myself. He also helps me accept the fact that by His power I can change. God expects me to admit that I do not control my own destiny. I need to realize that the Holy and Loving God of the Scriptures is the only Person I can trust to rule my life. God wants me to have the serenity of His presence as He takes control of my life and I trust in His love and generosity.

If I will only believe in God's willingness to work in me, He will give me a daily share in the resurrection power of His Son. Our Heavenly Father connected the resurrection of Jesus with the wonder-working power of God, by which He raised Jesus Christ from the dead. Such power God seeks to bestow upon me daily, if I will only admit my need of Him in prayer. Such power will sustain me in living for God—one day at a time.

Each day, I need to confess, prayerfully and humbly, my weakness and God's strength. Through this confession, I can have the confidence I need in the power of Jesus Christ to redeem me and restore my joy and serenity. If I trust God in prayer, God will fill me with His peace. God will give me confidence that His power in Jesus will give me the victory when I am tempted. He will give me peace beyond all expectation or understanding.

In my prayer fellowship with God, the Holy Spirit can fill me with the joy and victory that God won in the resurrection of Jesus Christ. In the midst of my temptations and trials, when I pray, Jesus will give me the power to overcome and succeed in life. Let the cross of Jesus Christ humble me to death, so God can work in me by His mighty Spirit and bring me to life, even everlasting life.

*Today's Date:*_____

Today's Requests:

Answers to Prayer and Thanksgivings:

The Second Step to Serenity

Reach Beyond Yourself

6

A Cure for My Anxiety

Do not be anxious about anything, but in everything, by prayer and petition, with thanksgiving, present your requests to God.

—Philippians 4:6

Without God, I am lost. I cannot concentrate on my real needs or overcome my problems. I cannot even pray. I try one thing and then another, but either I fail or they fail me. I used to keep picking myself up, but now I am sick and tired of falling again and again. I need a Power greater than me to give me healing and stability. I need the serenity that only God can give me in the midst of overwhelming worries.

God, help me to believe that only a real, continuous companionship with you will help me. Show me how prayer can become a daily life activity—moment by moment.

I want my dependence on my Higher Power to be just as natural as breathing or sleeping, not something I use just once or more a day, like some drug or an instant fix.

I will follow the principle of completely depending on God for everything. I will develop the holy habit of remembering that He is present with me each moment of the day. Since God is always near, I may call upon Him at all times. Eventually, my experiences with God will give me many good reasons to keep believing what the Bible teaches about not being anxious about anything.

I need to remember two things. God is always near, with His infinite and abundant grace ready to overcome my problems. In addition, I am utterly frail, and I must call upon Him to give me the power I need. I want to give the holy, gracious God all the time I can, so His light, life and love will fill my whole life. If I give Him time, through His Word and prayer, His love and peace will abide in me every day.

*Today's Date:*_____

Today's Requests:

Answers to Prayer and Thanksgivings:

The Second Step to Serenity

Reach Beyond Yourself

7

Overcoming My Greatest Stumbling Block

Come to me, all you who are weary and burdened, and I will give you rest.

—Matthew 11:28

My greatest stumbling block was the feeling I could never change. Old habits, emotional attachments, and the attractions of my surroundings had a strong pull upon me. Whenever I thought victory was out of reach, I also thought, "Why try?" Now I recognize that the change I needed was too difficult for me to make alone. I needed help.

Each day I need to ask God for the courage to believe that change and deliverance are possible for me. I need to ask Jesus for the courage to trust in Him. I need to tell Him that I am ready for Him to change me in any way that He decides is best for others and me. I must learn what total surrender means with respect to my relationship with God. When I think about the blessings others receive from total surrender, I can confidently give my life to Him.

If I feel satisfied maintaining a defective spiritual life, this will lead to my experiencing a defective prayer life. I truly want Jesus to free me from the power of sin, and give me a life of true faith and prayer! I pray for Jesus to give me victory over my unbelief, and then give me the courage and power to change.

Rather than follow the spirit of discouragement, I will place my faith in Jesus and choose to follow the spirit of gladness and hope.

God says to everyone, "Give yourself to Me. Believe that I will help you pray. Believe that I will give you transforming power. I strongly seek to pour My love into your heart! Be conscious of your lack of power, and then rely upon Me to give you grace and the power of prayer. I will cleanse you from all sin. I will deliver you from the sin of prayerlessness—only do not seek the victory in your own strength. Bow before Me as one who expects everything from his Savior. However sad or discouraged you may be, be assured of this—I will be gracious and give you a believing heart—I will teach you how to pray and how to change. I will give you serenity while the change you need takes effect in your life."

*Today's Date:*_____

Today's Requests:

Answers to Prayer and Thanksgivings:

Reach Beyond Yourself

8

Jesus Makes Me New

Therefore, if anyone is in Christ, he is a new creation; the old has gone, the new has come!

—2 Corinthians 5:17

For a long time I felt I had given God and Jesus a chance, but they had failed me. I was too impatient or too demanding, or I expected too much too quickly. Then, I found that my whole approach to and relationship with Jesus as my Lord and Savior had to be entirely new.

First, I came to understand that because of His infinite love, Jesus really does seek to have communion with me every moment of the day. With all His heart, Jesus longs for me to enjoy His companionship and His friendship.

Second, I came to believe in His divine power to conquer sin and keep me from falling. When I am tempted, if I look, I can find Jesus Christ providing the way of escape for me. Moreover, as He leads the way, He will give me the power I lack to follow Him out of trouble. With greater frequency, I now look to Jesus Christ in prayer when I encounter overpowering temptations. Through my experiences with Him, I know that only He can help me where I need help the most. Only His love can inspire me to love God and others more so I will want to avoid all sin and temptations.

Third, since Jesus is the Great Intercessor, I now know that He will fill me with joy, and through the Holy Spirit, He will give me the power to have daily communion with God in prayer. When I am in trouble, Jesus is praying in my behalf and His power will meet my needs and overcome my weaknesses.

Fourth, I have discovered that when I awake each morning I need to come to Jesus and surrender to Him once again. He will make me new each day. Therefore, at the dawning of every new day, I will ask Him to control completely my prayer life throughout the day.

My prayers are now becoming what God means them to be. Through the Spirit, my prayers are becoming the natural and joyful breathing of my spiritual life. In my communion with Jesus, I now inhale the heavenly atmosphere and exhale my prayers to God. Prayer and obedience have become as natural to me as failing in my weaknesses used to be. Spending time with God each day, surrendering my day to Him, has become a great joy for me and gives me the peace I need throughout the day!

*Today's Date:*_____

Today's Requests:

Answers to Prayer and Thanksgivings:

Reach Beyond Yourself

9

My Power from on High

I am going to send you what my Father has promised; but stay in the city until you have been clothed with power from on high.

—Luke 24:49

Why does Jesus pay attention to weak, powerless, helpless people like me? Because He knows that when I yield to Him and give Him the opportunity to rule as Lord in my heart, He can show His power to overcome in all things. He can conquer my weaknesses and temptations.

In the lives of His disciples, Jesus proves that His Father gave all power in heaven and on earth to Him. When Jesus sends the Holy Spirit to me as a powerful, personal presence within me, I cannot possess and use Him as I see fit or keep Him under my control. Just as Jesus lived and prayed on earth, so my responsibility is to pray, believe, and yield myself to my

Heavenly Father so the mighty power of God will work in me too. Jesus can prove in my life too that all power in heaven and on earth belongs to Him.

I want Jesus to make my whole attitude each day more prayerful, so His Spirit will influence me to lean with unceasing dependence upon Him. I need to pray daily with the confident expectation of receiving God's guidance and power in my life. God will guide me in the Scriptures as I study His teachings, and His Spirit will help me understand His word so it becomes life-changing truth for me each day.

Jesus' first disciples saw Him love and heal the sick, cast out demons and raise the dead. They saw His power over everything. They saw Him still the raging storm and give them peace. They received His teaching and saw His sufferings. They saw Him in His power and in His seeming weakness. However, in His weakness, they saw the power of God in His life. They saw Him raised from the dead, and they experienced His resurrection power in their hearts.

They also learned that without His living presence and power in their hearts each day, they were not able to make the truth about Him known to others in the right way. From His throne in heaven, Jesus had to take possession of them by His Spirit and dwell within them through His word.

Jesus longs to work wonders in my life. All I need to do is maintain my daily, prayerful, obedient contact with Him as my Holy and Almighty Friend.

*Today's Date:*_____

Today's Requests:

Answers to Prayer and Thanksgivings:

The Second Step to Serenity

Reach Beyond Yourself

10

The Secret of My Power in Prayer

> *If you love me, you will obey what I command. And I will ask the Father, and he will give you another Counselor to be with you forever—the Spirit of truth.*
>
> —John 14:15-17a

I will not be content with anything less than the indwelling life and power of the Holy Spirit in my heart. Unless Jesus works in me each day, I cannot live reasonably and have the power to overcome my trials, troubles and temptations. Through daily prayer, I can know that He is with me and at work in my life.

If I want God to restore me to substantial wholeness, I need the same devotion to Jesus that I see in His first disciples. The Lord Jesus asks for this loyalty from everyone who desires that He fill them with the power of His Spirit. God desires to fill me. In addition, Jesus wants me to receive His Spirit and power so I can pray and intercede for others more effectively, to link my needs with the needs of others in prayer, to bring blessings to others and myself.

To some, Jesus is something or nothing. To me, Jesus is everything. For those who do not know Him, Jesus is nothing. For the average believer, Jesus is something. For me, Jesus is everything. To receive the power of the Holy Spirit, I need to pray each day: "Lord Jesus, I yield myself with my whole heart this day to the leading of the Holy Spirit." A full surrender, a total letting go and letting God, is a matter life or death, sanity or insanity, an absolute necessity.

I have discovered that the mark of a true disciple is surrendering to God's love every day, all the day. True discipleship involves abiding in the Lord Jesus and keeping His commandments with a total reliance on His power and strength to help me obey no matter what the cost.

When I long to do God's will in everything, His love and Spirit rest upon me and give me serenity. In this spirit, I always find my secret power in prayer.

*Today's Date:*_____

Today's Requests:

Answers to Prayer and Thanksgivings:

Trust in God

11

Taking Time with God

There is a time for everything, and a season for every activity under heaven.

—Ecclesiastes 3: 1

God has given a time for everything—so why don't I spend more time in the presence of my Creator? Why don't I take the time to contemplate His will and purposes for me? Why don't I take time to measure my attitude and actions according to His revealed will in my reason, conscience, and the Bible?

My holy, loving God deserves the best of my time—of all my time. He merits the best in my life. I need to live in constant fellowship with God each day. To keep growing in faith, I must set aside a special time of quiet to be alone with God, to ask Him to examine and improve my life. In daily quiet times, I will ask God to show me what is best.

I need a daily period for secret fellowship with God. I need a quiet time for Him to shine the searchlight of His love into my heart, to reveal my hidden faults and intentions, the things I have done and left undone. I need a daily quiet time to turn from my occupations and search my heart in His presence. I need time to study His Word with reverence and godly fear. I need quiet time to seek His face and ask Him to make himself known to me. I need quiet time to wait until I know that He sees and hears me, so I can make my needs known to Him from the depth of my heart.

If I let God be God, and remember that I am only a creature, He will take His time to deal with my special needs. He will assure me of His forgiveness, cleanse me, and fill me with His mighty Spirit. If I let God take over the direction of my life, then God will show me what needs to be done and when. If I let God take control of my daily decisions, then He will show me how to live and give me the power to have the victory I seek when my weaknesses would otherwise pull me away into destructive attitudes and behaviors.

*Today's Date:*_____

Today's Requests:

Answers to Prayer and Thanksgivings:

Trust in God

12

Willing God's Will

Going a little farther, Jesus fell with his face to the ground and prayed, "My Father, if it is possible, may this cup be taken from me. Yet not as I will, but as you will."

—Matthew 26:39

To abide in unbroken fellowship with Christ and maintain ceaseless prayer to God, I need to surrender my life to Him every day, give myself over to His care, and ask Him to help me die to sin and the world.

Only Jesus can teach me what it means to turn my life over to His care and have fellowship with His sufferings. When He agonized in prayer on Gethsemane, He looked toward His death on the cross. God gave Him a vision of what it meant to die under the power of sin, and He prayed the cup might pass from Him. However, when He heard again the Father's will, He yielded up His whole will and life to God with the words: "Thy will be done." His whole life proved the power of praying, "God's will be done."

With these same words, I can enter into loving fellowship with God. With the words, "Thy will be done," Christ makes my heart strong and gives me confidence to believe that God will enable me, with Christ, to yield up everything to Him, to be "crucified with Christ," to overcome my problems and inherit eternal life.

"Let God's will be done." May this bold declaration be the deepest and the highest word in my life. May I use my daily quiet time to tell God with a full heart, "Let Your will be done." In the love of Christ and in the power of His Spirit, may this definite daily surrender to the will of God become the joy and strength of my prayerful obedience. May I experience the serenity that comes from a total submission to the will of God. May I enjoy everyday a prayerful submission that resolves when tempted to sin, "Let God's will be done. Let God's will be done in me and by me today."

*Today's Date:*_____

Today's Requests:

Answers to Prayer and Thanksgivings:

Trust in God

13

From My Strength to God's

Blessed are those whose strength is in you, who have set their hearts on pilgrimage. They go from strength to strength, till each appears before God in Zion.

—Psalm 84:5, 7

When I cling to God's promises in the Bible, He assures me of His unfailing love and faithfulness through Jesus my Lord. When my spiritual growth goes slowly, I can thank God for the promises He has made to me in His word. Through the indwelling Spirit, I go from strength to strength. God's Truth and Holy Spirit give me the assurance that He will perfect His work in me daily. Through prayer, I have learned to rely wholly upon God's grace.

God closely connected the Holy Spirit with our prayer life. We receive the Holy Spirit after repenting of our sins and confessing our faith in

Jesus. Still, the Spirit life requires a continuous prayer life. If we continually give ourselves to prayer, then the Spirit can lead us continually. As we submit ourselves to the Spirit's control, we can avoid destructive behavior and bring happiness to others.

Am I willing to decide today to turn myself over to the care of God? Am I willing to reaffirm this decision daily? Am I willing to ask God to take control every time I want to follow my feelings and return to my old ways of living?

God wants to accomplish a great deal in my life, but my spending time in prayer and in fellowship with God is indispensable for God to work fully in my life. Jesus Christ revealed that if I open my heart and mouth toward heaven, He would not fail me or put me to shame.

To obtain God's blessings, I must pray. I must entirely surrender my heart and life to Him. I must believe in the power of prayer. I rest now with the assurance that God will care for me and work powerfully in me as I turn my life over to Him, and do so daily in prayer.

*Today's Date:*_____

Today's Requests:

Answers to Prayer and Thanksgivings:

Trust in God

14

The Spirit Will Pray for Me

In the same way, the Spirit helps us in our weakness. We do not know what we ought to pray for, but the Spirit himself intercedes for us with groans that words cannot express.

—Romans 8:26

If God left me to myself, I would not know how to pray. God stooped down and rescued me in my helplessness by giving me the Holy Spirit to pray for me. The work of the Holy Spirit in every believer's life is deeper than human thoughts or feelings. God hears the Spirit in our prayers in ways beyond our understanding.

The Holy Spirit teaches what the Bible means about God. The Holy Spirit works in us so we can turn our lives over to God and receive His care. The Holy Spirit helps us humbly admit that any moral improvement or spiritual progress we make comes primarily from God's work in us.

Before I turned my life over to God, He worked upon me from the outside. If He used me at all, I was no better spiritually. I was like a lifeless metal saw in the hand of a master carpenter. Now, as a believer in Jesus Christ, His Spirit works with a mighty power inside me. From the inside, the Holy Spirit gives me power to change. From the inside, the Holy Spirit inspires me to make choices that will bless others as well as me. The Spirit leads me to offer myself willingly to the Master for His perfect purposes. The Holy Spirit works from the inside out, so others can also enjoy the fruits of my Christ-centered life.

Because I have turned my life over to God, I can come into His presence with the confidence that the Holy Spirit will carry out His work in my prayers. Such confidence will inspire reverence and quietness, and will enable me to depend on the Holy Spirit to present my needs and desires to God in a way that He will accept. Through the Holy Spirit, my prayers will have more value than I can imagine. No wonder the serenity I feel today is from the Holy Spirit's work in me.

In every prayer of the believer, the Triune God participates. God the Father hears our prayers. We pray in the name of His Son, so He will answer our prayers. Moreover, the Holy Spirit prays in us and for us about the things we need. When we turn our lives over to the Triune God, we know that God will hear our prayers and meet our needs.

*Today's Date:*_____

Today's Requests:

Answers to Prayer and Thanksgivings:

Trust in God

15

Thanking God for His Care

> *I will pour out on the house of David and the inhabitants of Jerusalem a spirit of grace and supplication. They will look on me, the one they have pierced, and they will mourn for him as one mourns for an only child, and grieve bitterly for him as one grieves for a firstborn son.*
>
> —Zechariah 12:10

Today, I thank God for the certain promise that He will care for me now that I have turned my life over to Him. I reckon, with full assurance of faith, that through the Holy Spirit, God now indwells me as His Temple.

The Bible calls the Holy Spirit the "spirit of grace and supplication." He now dwells within me to rule my life with His gentle and loving guidance; therefore, I have power to become a new person. I thank God when I pray and ask His Spirit to fill me with ever more reasons to praise and thank God for His blessings. Thanksgiving in prayer draws my heart closer to God and keeps me consciously aware of His loving care for others and me.

Without prayer, I found the work of trying to live the Christian life too hard. At first, I tried to have fellowship with God as I imagined Him to be, but that did not work. When I tried to pray apart from the Holy Spirit's help, I found that communion with God was impossible without the Holy Spirit praying for me.

The Holy Spirit reveals the Father and the Son to us, and glorifies the Son. When I turned my life over to the care of Jesus, the Holy Spirit made such changes in me that Jesus received all the praise and thanksgiving for any blessings He bestowed on others through me. The Scriptures reveal that God wants Jesus to receive the glory and honor for our victories. With a willingly heart, I give God all the credit for any improvements I make in my life.

The Spirit of Holiness teaches me to recognize hate, and turn from evil. The Spirit shows me where I still feel resentments against others, so I can forgive them. The Spirit teaches me how to pray for my enemies. The Spirit helps me turn from fear and fills me with the peace of God. When I came to understand that the Holy Spirit is the Spirit of Wisdom, Love, and Power, I more readily committed myself to His daily guidance and care.

*Today's Date:*_____

Today's Requests:

Answers to Prayer and Thanksgivings:

Examine Your Life

16

The Root Cause of My Problems

If we claim to be without sin, we deceive ourselves and the truth is not in us.

—1 John 1:8

I am searching for the root cause of my character defects, and for any reasons within me for my problems. I need to direct my attention to my character defects, or secondary influences and problems will always plague me and I will never have the healing I seek.

Through prayer, God will give me proper insight into my true character and help me see myself as He sees me and perhaps as others see me. I need to stop fooling myself and misleading others. As I begin to list the wrongs I have done, I will overcome the deadness and failure I feel sometimes in my private prayers. As I begin to deal with my problems and their root causes, I will not blame my lack of fellowship with God on God.

What is the root cause of my problems and my failure to hear from God? Is it selfishness and self-centeredness? Do most of my shortcomings have their origin in my obsessive self-concern? Have all of my prayers focused on the things I want from God and others? Oh God, help me to recognize this evil and forever renounce it. By your grace, help me put you first in my life, and make room in my heart for you and others.

Just two things are possible: walking with the Holy Spirit according to the Scriptures, or following my selfish desires and feelings. Oh God, fill me with your Holy Spirit, so I will not fulfill the compulsions and desires that harm others or me. Open my mind so I can understand the scriptures; then, I will know what to do when temptations, compulsions, and unholy desires assault me. Then I will experience the serenity I seek—all day and every day!

*Today's Date:*_____

Today's Requests:

Answers to Prayer and Thanksgivings:

Examine Your Life

17

God Reveals My Problems the Best

If we walk in the light, as God is in the light, we have fellowship with one another, and the blood of Jesus, his Son, purifies us from all sin.

—1 John 1:7

If I am to understand more fully the grace of God, and how His Son can help me, I need to recognize my character defects. As I prayerfully read the Word of God, the Holy Spirit will shine His light, give me understanding, and apply God's Word to the defects in my life. The Bible will teach me how horrible sin and its consequences are, and this truth will motivate me to avoid it. Such daily, prayerful reading and asking God to point out my sins in the light of His Word takes courage that only the Holy Spirit can give me.

I thank God that the Holy Spirit will not show me all of my character defects at once. Through His gentle, loving Spirit, God will show me only what He knows I can bear and deal with each day—at-the-moment. God does not seek to condemn me, but to save me from the misery and unhappiness my defects cause.

If others try to be the Holy Spirit for me, the pain and shame of admitting my character defects may be more than I can bear. If I try to take the moral inventory of others, I may influence them to avoid their pain and run away from their problems or return to their destructive behaviors.

I am prayerfully working through these prayer steps to serenity so God can gently show me my problems and give me His remedy. I cannot allow myself to think that daily sin is a necessity and cease to mourn over my sins. I will make spiritual progress only if I bring my actions before my conscious mind, evaluate them, and confess to God in prayer every transgression against God, others and myself each day.

*Today's Date:*_____

Today's Requests:

Answers to Prayer and Thanksgivings:

The Fourth Step to Serenity

Examine Your Life

18

The Problem of Prayerlessness

As for me, far be it from me that I should sin against the Lord by failing to pray for you.

—1 Samuel 12:23

The sin of prayerlessness can have a terrible effect. In saying my prayers, I can actually not be praying at all. If I deceive myself and do not get better, I can begin to distrust God and prayer. Prayerlessness can be a hasty and superficial communion with God, a hurrying to get on with "more important things."

Just saying my prayers everyday will not help me hate sin or give me the power to flee from temptations. Praying needs to be more than just saying words, saying the same words over and over again. When I just "say" my prayers, I give my hand over to Satan and his power. Can I take time to pray to God with my whole heart? If I want to stay close to God and receive the serenity He wants to give me, can I do anything less than give my heart to God?

As God's child, I am slowly learning more about prayer, and that nothing but hidden, humble, constant fellowship with God can teach me to hate sin, as God wants me to hate it. As I open my hidden life to God, He will help me hate sin and give me the hope of overcoming my flaws. Only by maintaining a constant nearness to the living Lord Jesus will He give me unceasing power to understand how to detest and conquer my character defects and weaknesses.

As God's Truth and Spirit reveal my sins to me, I need to develop a deeper understanding of prayer and God's willingness to grant me pardon. When I look to Jesus and meditate on what it cost Him to forgive, purify and renew me, He gives me power and works out the victory over temptation that would destroy my peace with God and others. He fills me with peace. He bestows in me the real peace of God with His very presence in me.

I can never repay the Lord Jesus for His gift of love to me, but I can linger longer in His presence and express my love and gratitude with words of praise. As I praise Him, I will become more like Him, and His holiness will rest upon me.

*Today's Date:*_____

Today's Requests:

Answers to Prayer and Thanksgivings:

Examine Your Life

19

The One Who Can Save Me

She will give birth to a son, and you are to give him the name Jesus, because he will save his people from their sins.

—Matthew 1:21

As I begin to confess my sins to God, so He can cleanse my heart and my accusing conscience, I need to list the things I have done to harm others and myself. As I do this, I need to remember that the Lord Jesus Christ will forgive me and save me from my transgressions. The name Jesus means Savior.

As His follower, Jesus wants me to love and adore Him each day. Have I done this? If not, have I put this on my list of wrongs? Does my list include dishonoring God, dishonoring myself, and dishonoring others?

Through daily communion with Jesus, He will save me from my sins. He will reveal himself to me, and through the power of His love, He will cast out my love for sin. He will save me from my trespasses by the power of daily personal fellowship with Him. He will show me the way to escape the temptations that I almost love to seek, even though I feel worse every time I fall.

If I want salvation from my sins, I need to bring my heart to Jesus, even with the sin that is in it, and ask Him to be my almighty personal Savior. He can save me from every sin in my list of moral defects. As Jesus and I spend more time together and express our mutual love for one another, by the work of His Holy Spirit in my heart, His love will expel and conquer every sin within me.

I need to learn the blessedness of maintaining fellowship with Jesus each day. Communion with Jesus is the secret of all true happiness and holiness. As I do this more and more, my heart will long for the hour of prayer, because it will be the best hour of the day.

As I spend time alone with Jesus, I will experience His presence enabling me to love Him, serve Him, and walk in His ways. Through unbroken fellowship with a holy God, I will have the secret power of a truly holy life.

*Today's Date:*_____

Today's Requests:

Answers to Prayer and Thanksgivings:

The Fourth Step to Serenity

Examine Your Life

20

My Reason for Rejoicing

Jesus said, "Father, forgive them, for they do not know what they are doing." And they divided up his clothes by casting lots.

—Luke 23:34

As I continue working on my list of character defects, I rejoice that God loves me in spite of what I have done. God loves His enemies as well as His friends. Just as Jesus prayed for His enemies as He hung on the cross, I know He is praying for me as I make a list of the wrongs I have committed. He died for me, and now from heaven He intercedes for me and rejoices as I seek wholeness.

Jesus calls me to love my enemies too, to pray for them and bless them. As I think of those who influenced me to do wrong, I am tempted to hold a grudge against them or even hate them. As I think about these people, I need to forgive them just as Jesus forgives me. Hanging on to old resentments will only hinder my spiritual growth and keep me from having the close communion with God that I need through prayer.

When I think of the repentant thief who prayed to Jesus for mercy as he hung upon the cross, I marvel at the wonderful love of God. I rejoice in Jesus' readiness to forgive and the joy He must have felt when He said, "I tell you the truth, today you will be with me in paradise" (Luke 23:43). I trust in God's ready forgiveness, and this faith inspires me to keep on examining my life thoroughly. I know that through fearless self-examination, as Jesus gives me the assurance of His forgiving love, I can enjoy the serenity that daily meditation and prayer can give me.

The cross of Jesus Christ is a cross of love. I owe my future to the sacrificial, redeeming love of God. As I pray to God and confess my errors and trespasses, I know that He will forgive me and enable me to follow Him more nearly each day. As I see the progress I make daily, I will rejoice in His love. As others see the changes God makes in me daily, they will see the depth and power of God's life-transforming love and truth.

*Today's Date:*_____

Today's Requests:

Answers to Prayer and Thanksgivings:

Admit Your Mistakes

21

Conscience and Confession

If we confess our sins, he is faithful and just and will forgive us our sins and purify us from all unrighteousness.

—1 John 1:9

For my conscience to work as God intended, I must truly repent of the wrongs I have done. I must confess my outward actions (that others probably know about), and the hidden thoughts that have prompted me to act in ways that were harmful. To find happiness and wholeness, to find freedom from the power of my wrecked past, I must list and confess each individual sin and shortcoming by name. I must be intensely personal as I pray to God and ask His forgiveness.

How wonderful to think that my holy God invites me, an unworthy sinner, to come to Him for the assurance of forgiveness and fellowship. He invites me to experience the depth of companionship with Him that the forgiven enjoy. He created me in His image. He redeemed me by His Son, so I can have salvation from the power of sin and enjoy everlasting life with Him. How wonderful to realize that God has provided the solution to my every problem. Surely, God does not want any sin that I have failed to confess to stand in the way of a blessed and glorious relationship with Him.

When I am sick, I try to discover the true cause of my illness and the best way to treat it. With some illnesses, I need a doctor to diagnose my problem and give me the treatment I need. When I confess my trespasses to a trustworthy person, he can give me the treatment I need: the assurance of forgiveness. To find serenity and peace with God and others, I must take this important step. The cause of many of my problems is the burden of the sins that I carry and have not confessed. God has promised that if I take time to confess every sin, He will forgive me and cleanse me from all my corruptions. After confessing my sins, I will know deep within my heart that the smiling face of God is upon me when I pray.

*Today's Date:*_____

Today's Requests:

Answers to Prayer and Thanksgivings:

Admit Your Mistakes

22

Life Follows Death to Self

> *I tell you the truth, unless a kernel of wheat falls to the ground and dies, it remains only a single seed. But if it dies, it produces many seeds.*
>
> —John 12:24

Every seed teaches me how I will receive a beautiful and fruitful life by dying to self. Confession kills pride and brings forth the beautiful fruit of humility. God gives grace to the humble. Jesus had to pass through death in all its bitterness and suffering before He could rise to heaven and impart His life to those He redeemed. I must learn the lesson of self-sacrifice. I must die to the self-life.

When I admit my shortcomings to God and another human being, I die inside. However, the death of pride will lead me to new life, peace of mind, and the assurance of God's accepting and forgiving love.

I once wondered, "Did Jesus really need to die?" Yes, He did. God laid upon Him the evil deeds of us all, and Jesus yielded His life to the Father so through His death we might have life. Jesus' death made our forgiveness and new life possible. I need to accept Jesus' death for me personally. Since He died for all, He died for me. I need to take that fact to heart and live my life with the conscious understanding that He gave His life for me.

As I confess my inner bondage to many evil things, through my fellowship with Christ and His cross, I will die to my preoccupation with self and He will free me to live for God and others. My prayers will become God-centered instead of self-centered. With joy and eagerness, I will learn to obey His call to bear my cross and die daily. In every prayer, I will see myself as "crucified with Christ." Knowing that Jesus works within me will inspire me to die daily and gladly the death to self and selfishness that will bring me into fellowship with Him and give me new life.

The Spirit of Christ Jesus, the Risen Lord, can make His death and life my daily experience. In yielding submissive prayer, Jesus will give me power to overcome temptation and conquer every spiritual enemy. Through submissive prayer, I will find the serenity I seek.

*Today's Date:*_____

Today's Requests:

Answers to Prayer and Thanksgivings:

Admit Your Mistakes

23

God's Forgiveness Inspires My Love

The LORD, the LORD, the compassionate and gracious God, slow to anger, abounding in love and faithfulness, maintaining love to thousands, and forgiving wickedness, rebellion and sin.

—Exodus 34:6, 7

Until a person really confesses his sins to God, he cannot understand how abundantly God forgives. Through confessing my sins, I will come to know by experience the riches of God's mercy. By His faithfulness and abounding love, God has led me to the point of being ready to admit to Him the exact nature of my wrongs. I cannot doubt that His compassion and grace are also able to forgive me and restore me to fellowship with Him. Confession will remove all the barriers between God and me, and my prayers will be completely unhindered. True confession leads to true communion.

Through understanding more of God's character, His hatred of sin and His love for humankind, the fact that He is holy yet slow to anger, I will come to love Him more. The secret of maintaining the openness with God that I seek is being willing to confess any sins I commit each day. As I confess my shortcomings and seek His cleansing from all unrighteousness, I will keep my heart clean. As I meet with God each day, I will live in the light of His love. I have learned the secret to success in prayer: I need to draw near to God with absolute surrender to His will and desire to know and walk in His ways each day.

I know with assurance that God forgives and will forgive me when I admit my wrongs. I now approach the Throne of Grace with boldness. I bow before my loving, holy, and Heavenly Father. In humble adoration, I learn more about effective prayer—prayer that receives the answer it seeks.

*Today's Date:*_____

Today's Requests:

Answers to Prayer and Thanksgivings:

Admit Your Mistakes

24

God Will Forgive My Prayerlessness

When you pray, go into your room, close the door and pray to your Father, who is unseen. Then your Father, who sees what is done in secret, will reward you.

—Matthew 6:6

No one other than God needs to know the exact nature of my wrongs. Nevertheless, after I also confidentially confessed my shortcomings to a trusted advisor, I received the freeness and openness I needed to pray to God in secret. As I spend more and more time with God, He will make such a difference in my life that others will openly see the rewards of walking with God and doing so in constant prayer and reliance upon Him.

The Lord Jesus, the one who saves us from our sins, is able and willing to deliver me from all sin. He will deliver me from the sin of prayerlessness and of failing to spend time with Him in secret prayer. To experience this deliverance, I must acknowledge and confess in a childlike and simple way the sin of not using a private place of prayer. Almost all of my problems have come from failing to spend time with God and asking God to lead me, free me from evil, and empower me to do all the good I can to those around me. With deep sorrow and shame, I need to confess my failure to spend quality time with God in prayer and meditation upon His Word.

I need to confess that I was deceived in thinking that I could solve my problems and get through life in my own strength. I need to confess that I thought I could pray, as I ought to pray, without needing any help from the Holy Spirit. I need to confess that the power of the world and my self-confidence led me astray and that I do not have the strength to do better alone.

If I will confess these things with all my heart, God will give me wonderful success as I continue stepping out with faith in Him and with a desire to know and do His will. As He has promised, I can do all things through Jesus Christ who strengthens me.

*Today's Date:*_____

Today's Requests:

Answers to Prayer and Thanksgivings:

The Fifth Step to Serenity

Admit Your Mistakes

25

My Forgiveness Brings Singing

I acknowledged my sin to you and did not cover up my iniquity. I said, "I will confess my transgressions to the Lord"—and you forgave the guilt of my sin.

—Psalm 32:5

Confession can be superficial. Honest confession gives power over sin. In fellowship with the Lord Jesus Christ, I need to confess every sin with an open and sincere heart, for every sin will hinder victorious faith and living.

Once, King David was unwilling to confess his sins, but then he learned: "When I kept silent, my bones wasted away through my groaning all day long. For day and night, your hand was heavy upon me; my strength was sapped as in the heat of summer. Then I acknowledged my sin to you and did not cover up my iniquity. I said, 'I will confess my transgressions to the LORD'—and you forgave the guilt of my sin" (Ps 32:3-5). He also discovered that after confession God filled him with gratitude and surrounded him with "songs of deliverance" (Psalm 32:7). He found the forgiveness and serenity he sought, and this led him to sing his songs of glorious praise.

When God chastens or disciplines me, He does so to save me from sin, now and forever. When I return to God and confess, all heaven rejoices. Jesus said, "I tell you, there is rejoicing in the presence of the angels of God over one sinner who repents" (Luke 15:10) And, "I tell you that in the same way there is more rejoicing in heaven over one sinner who repents than over ninety-nine righteous persons who do not need to repent" (Luke 15:7). I must not neglect to confess my sins in prayer!

When I confess my sin with shame, I also hand it over to God. I trust God to take it away. Confessing my sins reminds me that I am unable to rid myself of my guilt by myself. I must act in faith that God will deliver me through the precious promises Jesus Christ has made to those who repent.

As I continue working through these prayer steps to serenity, I will discover two truths by experience. First, I will know that God has forgiven my sins. Second, I will learn that Jesus is cleansing me from my sins and keeping me from falling. As I seek fellowship with Jesus each day through prayer, I need not fear confessing my sins. I pray to Him in the confident assurance that He will forgive and deliver me from all my sins and temptations.

*Today's Date:*_____

Today's Requests:

Answers to Prayer and Thanksgivings:

The Sixth Step to Serenity

Transform Your Thinking

26

God Will Remove My Fear

That we being delivered out of the hands of our enemies should serve Him without fear, in holiness and righteousness, before Him, all our days.
—Luke 1:74, 75—KJV

I am my own greatest enemy. My own character defects and shortcomings can cause me far greater harm than anyone else can. However, these need not ruin the rest of my life. God can remove them, and then fill the vacancies they leave with His holy presence. Am I ready to have God remove my defects of character, or do I want to live with the continual fear that my actions may someday destroy others as well as me?

If I humbly bow before the Lord Jesus Christ and ask Him to rule in my life, He will remove my shortcomings and fill me with His loving Spirit. Thank God for Jesus Christ living in me by grace through faith.

Through the Holy Spirit, Jesus will dwell in me and give me the power to keep from doing evil. Through Jesus abiding in me, I will have the desire and the power to do God's will in all things. Think of the inspired words of Zacharias, quoted above, as he prophesied the deliverance that the Lord Jesus Christ would bring. As we serve Jesus Christ, we have no reason to fear Him. These are the words of God, and they show what He will do for those who seek Him.

God's promises are sure, and He fulfills them in those who wholeheartedly and confidently claim them. Claim this promise for yourself today: "I will sprinkle clean water on you, and you will be clean; I will cleanse you from all your impurities and from all your idols. And I will put my Spirit in you and move you to follow my decrees and be careful to keep my laws. I the LORD have spoken, and I will do it (Ezekiel 36:25, 27, 36b).

Today's Date:_____

Today's Requests:

Answers to Prayer and Thanksgivings:

The Sixth Step to Serenity

Transform Your Thinking

27

Jesus Promises to Transform Me

Trust in God; trust also in me. You may ask me for anything in my name, and I will do it.

—John 14:1, 14

When I receive Jesus Christ as my Lord and Savior, God will grant me all the fullness of His redeeming grace. Through fellowship with Jesus, I will enjoy redemption day by day. A close, daily fellowship with Jesus will keep me from slipping back into my old ways. Jesus living in me makes it possible for me to persevere in a loving, powerful, prayerful, life of obedience.

In Jesus, God promises to remove all my defects of character. In my morning prayers, I can begin and maintain an intimate, spiritual, personal and uninterrupted relationship with my Lord throughout the day. In addition, He will manifest himself with great power in my life. In the

Lord Jesus, all the attributes of God will work powerfully within me and morally transform me. When I ask Jesus to remove my character defects, He will do it. Then daily fellowship with Him in prayer will give me the power I need to overcome every temptation to return to my old destructive ways.

As the glorified Son of God, Jesus' presence can fill me at all times, and give me the power I need to live a transformed life. As a disciple of Jesus, I need to learn this lesson: "The Lord loves me so, that He wants me near Him without a break, so I can experience His love." Every time I feel powerless to change, I need to remind myself of His ever-present love for me and within me. Remembering this will give me power in prayer, as I pray for those I love, others in my fellowship and church, as well as myself.

When I commit myself to living with the Lord Jesus Christ for the whole day, His eternal, almighty power will protect me and accomplish every good thing. When I take time for prayer, I will experience in full reality the presence of the Almighty Jesus!

*Today's Date:*_____

Today's Requests:

Answers to Prayer and Thanksgivings:

The Sixth Step to Serenity

Transform Your Thinking

28

I Can Become More Like God

> *I am the Lord your God; consecrate yourselves and be holy, because I am holy.*
>
> —Leviticus 11:44

I need to learn how to give God and His holiness the place He deserves in my faith and life. To practice God's Holy Presence, I need to read God's Holy Word with deep humility as I pray.

In the Book of Leviticus, God commands us five times, "Be holy, for I am holy." The Apostle Paul prays for all believers: "May God strengthen your hearts so that you will be blameless and holy in the presence of our God and Father when our Lord Jesus comes with all his holy ones. For God did not call us to be impure, but to live a holy life. The one who calls you is faithful and he will do it" (1 Thessalonians 3:13; 4:7; 5:24). God will make me holy, like Him.

Only by knowing God as the Holy One will I become holy. I will not obtain this knowledge of God unless I spend some time alone with Him in prayer. I need to take time for the holiness of God to shine on me. His holiness in me will empower me to live wholly for Him and others instead of primarily for myself.

How can anyone obtain intimate knowledge of a person with extraordinary wisdom unless he associates with that person and remains under his influence? Likewise, how can God make me holy, if I will not take time to come under the power of His glory and holiness? Only through prayer and meditation upon the Word of God can I come under the power and influence of God and get to know His Holiness personally in me. As I study His Word, He speaks divine truth to my heart and soul. Someone has said, "No one can expect to make progress in holiness if he is not often and long alone with God."

Holiness may be the most profound word in the Bible. John heard the four living creatures call out: "Holy, holy, holy is the Lord God Almighty" (Revelation 4:8). By simply thinking, reading and hearing, I will not understand or partake in the Holiness of God. I need to be alone with God and pray: "Let your Holiness, O Lord, shine more and more into my heart that I may become holy like you." His Spirit will use the truth to transform my life and give me the constant serenity I so desperately need as He makes me holy.

*Today's Date:*_____

Today's Requests:

Answers to Prayer and Thanksgivings:

The Sixth Step to Serenity

Transform Your Thinking

29

Receiving the Fullness of God

Your attitude should be the same as that of Christ Jesus
—Philippians 2:5

Because Jesus humbled himself and obeyed God, His Heavenly Father, to the death, even death on a cross, His Father exalted Him. Above everything else, the obedient spirit of Jesus needs to become the chief characteristic of my disposition. I need to pray for Jesus' attitude toward life and death, and ask Him to give me His viewpoint on everything.

As I prepare to ask God to remove all of my character defects, am I also willing to obey God in all things? Could my major character defect turn out to be my unwillingness to try to obey God in everything? Am I really willing to pray, "O God, help me always to do your will"?

An employee who habitually disobeyed his boss and hurt others would lose his job. Likewise, as a child of God, I should not habitually disobey God. Should God treat me any differently from the way an honest employer would treat a dishonest employee out to do harm to others and himself? If I just confessed the same trespasses repeatedly everyday, and did not surrender to God and pray for God to remove my character defects, how should I expect God to treat me? God has always been far more loving and gracious than I deserve. Can I admit this fact and love Him even more for His grace?

The Holy Spirit desires to possess me fully. To receive the fullness of His loving presence, I need to surrender fully to His rule. The Scriptures command me to follow the Spirit's leading and walk by the Spirit. To have a right relationship to the Holy Spirit, I need to pray for His constant guidance and rule over my life. Obeying God from a heart full of love is the most important factor in my whole relationship to God.

It is one thing for me to want to overcome those habits, addictions, compulsions, weaknesses, and dependencies that are destroying me, and quite another thing for me to be ready to obey God in all things. What is this difference? It involves my choosing to turn from self-centeredness to God-centeredness. It involves my decision to quit living in selfishness and begin living in loving-kindness toward God and others, the loving-kindness of God's grace in me. Once I make this decision and pray for the power of Christ to work powerfully in me, God will help me find the victory I seek over addictions, compulsions, dependencies, and weaknesses.

*Today's Date:*_____

Today's Requests:

Answers to Prayer and Thanksgivings:

Transform Your Thinking

30

Prayer Leads Me to Victory

What a wretched man I am! Who will rescue me from this body of death? Thanks be to God—through Jesus Christ our Lord.
—Romans 7:24, 25

My way of living has a mighty influence over my prayers. If I am worldly and self-seeking, my prayers will be powerless and unanswered. Is there a conflict between my life and prayer? Am I ready for God to make any changes He finds necessary, so my prayers will be more effective? Am I ready to have every character defect removed? Am I ready to avoid every situation and flee from every opportunity that will tempt me to do wrong?

I cannot allow the ways of the world to have the upper hand in my life. I need God to rule and exercise His mighty influence over me. Prayer can conquer sin. Through prayer, God can show me the way to escape or overcome every temptation I face. In prayer, I will yield myself completely to God. I will bring my entire life under the control of God through prayer. If I receive the Lord Jesus Christ into my life, then through prayer He will change and renew my life. He will purify and sanctify me.

If I am not ready for God to remove my character defects, the rest of my prayer life will be defective. I will be working myself up to pray more and more, and will be disappointed at the results. Only as God strengthens my spiritual life, through my daily surrender to Him, will my prayer time joyfully increase. God will not allow me to disconnect my way of living from the way I pray.

Which has more influence over me: a five-minute prayer or my worldly desires? If my prayer life and my desires compete with each other, then I may be concentrating more on fulfilling my desires than obeying God. If I give God total control and surrender my heart to Him, then prayer will come to rule my life. After I ask God to take full possession of my heart and life, prayer will become as sacred and powerful as God wants it to be.

*Today's Date:*_____

Today's Requests:

Answers to Prayer and Thanksgivings:

The Seventh Step to Serenity

Remove Your Defects

31

God's Wonderful Promises to Me

For I will forgive their wickedness and will remember their sins no more.

—Hebrews 8:12

The Lord Jesus Christ died to atone for my sins. By His grace through faith, He will destroy the power of sin over my life. He came to give me free access to God's presence. Therefore, in His Name I can secure God's favor when I pray. He came to remove my shortcomings and give me a new heart. He freed me from the power of sin, and filled me with the Holy Spirit. The Spirit now breathes in me the power to obey God in all things.

I will put my trust in Jesus Christ for the forgiveness of my sins and claim the fullness of His other promise—that He will remove all my shortcomings. He will remove them. He will cleanse me. He will give me the victory when I am tempted to sin once again. He will give me such a delight in and love for God's law that I will rejoice in all God's commandments. God will give me such power in prayer that I will focus more on Him and others than on myself.

I have come a long way from breaking the rules and ignoring the consequences. I now see why all of God's standards are right and reasonable, and that I need Him to remove my defects of character so I can do right. If I ask Him, Jesus will write God's law on my heart by the power of His Spirit so I will know how to act in every situation. His Spirit within me will show me how to truly love and serve others in the power of God.

God asked Abraham "Is anything too hard for the Lord?" (Genesis 18:14). If I will set aside my preconceived opinions and believe in the almighty power of God and His desire to help me, He will remove my shortcomings and give me serenity in the face of every challenge and obstacle I have yet to encounter.

*Today's Date:*_____

Today's Requests:

Answers to Prayer and Thanksgivings:

The Seventh Step to Serenity

Remove Your Defects

32

God Will Work Wonders in Me

I pray that out of his glorious riches he may strengthen you with power through his Spirit in your inner being, so that Christ may dwell in your hearts through faith.

—Ephesians 3:16, 17

Only the God who works wonders can help me. If I ask Him in faith, He will remove all my shortcomings. If I lack love, I can go to the Throne of Grace, and He will fill me with His love. God is love. Whatever I really need, He will see that I have.

The gift of love comes when Jesus fills my heart with His presence. As I seek God in prayer, Jesus will sustain my love for Him. As Jesus dwells more fully in me, He will remove all of my shortcomings. When I humbly bow before the Throne of Grace and humbly wait and worship there, I will receive the indwelling Spirit and know the love of Christ in me.

I do not seek forgiveness only. I also seek that abundant grace that will help me to be continually victorious over my temptations. During my time in prayer and meditation on the Word of God, I ask God to fit me for the continual indwelling and guidance of the Holy Spirit. I earnestly pray that I may so live that the love of Christ, which passes all understanding, will be first place in my life. Only by spending time before the Throne of Grace will I root and ground my life and healing in the almighty love of God.

When I have come to really love God and have gotten beyond just talking about my need to love Him, His love will radiate from me to all those around. The love of Christ in me will reach out and enrich the hearts of those who do not yet know Him, love Him, or follow Him. By grace, through faith and prayer, I will obtain the blessedness I seek: the serenity that sometimes eludes me.

Today's Date:_____

Today's Requests:

Answers to Prayer and Thanksgivings:

Remove Your Defects

33

God's Love Will Remove My Hatred

My command is this: Love each other as I have loved you.
—John 15:12

I have found that Jesus' command to love is so difficult to keep that I am often tempted to quit trying. Some people have done some very hateful things to others and me. Yet, the prayer steps to serenity require that I recognize my own hateful attitudes as shortcomings and character defects that God needs to remove and that I can change with God's help. In my Quiet Time, I will ask God to help me overcome any hatred or unforgivingness that I still harbor in my heart or thoughts.

Jesus loves me and fills me with His love. As I open more of my heart to Him, He will fill me even more. He dwells within me and will cast out my character defects—if I humbly ask Him. Day-by-day, if I ask Him to remove my destructive attitudes, compulsions and feelings, I will improve and learn to pray even for my enemies. As I spend more time with Jesus, I gradually begin to take on His loving and forgiving character.

If I say I love God and hate my brother, I am a liar. If I hate my fellow-man, this is a sure sign I do not truly love God. To hate and to love are choices I make, not just feelings I nurture, and I cannot at the same time love God and hate God's children.

Jesus really means, "Love one another as I have loved you." Through the Holy Spirit, that He sends to live in every believer, He will enable me to love others. As I love others in the power of Jesus' love, they will also grow strong in love. As they grow strong in love, I will have powerful evidence that Jesus dwells in me and the Father has shed His love abroad in my heart.

I want to bow at the Throne of Jesus. I want to love, worship and adore Him for His wonderful grace. By His love, He seeks to transform me and make me more like himself. As He lives in my heart, He will cast out hatred, give me a wonderful love for others, and prove to the world that God is definitely in our midst.

*Today's Date:*_____

Today's Requests:

Answers to Prayer and Thanksgivings:

The Seventh Step to Serenity

Remove Your Defects

34

My Whole Life Depends on Jesus

Do not let your hearts be troubled. Trust in God; trust also in me.
—John 14:1

The Bible teaches that Jesus taught His disciples to pray to and believe in Him with the same perfect confidence they had in God the Father. I need to ask God to remove those flaws in me that influence me to visualize a god compatible with my character defects. If I imagine or even serve a god with moral defects instead of the perfect God, I may comfort my conscience until it no longer will speak to me of my wrongs. However, if I am to ready change for the better, I need to ask God to remake me into His moral image—into the perfect image of His Son, the Son of His perfect love.

The deity of Jesus is the rock upon which my faith depends. The Lord Jesus, as a man, partook of my nature, but without any defects of character or moral flaws. He lived without sin. He is indeed true God. Divine power raised Jesus from the dead, and His divine omnipotence can work in me to overcome my weaknesses.

I need to humble myself and ask Jesus to remove any character defects in me. I do not want any character defects to keep me from seeing God as He is. Jesus said, "Blessed are the pure in heart for they will see God" (Matthew 6:8). As Jesus removes my flaws and creates a pure heart within me, I will see God as He really is, and I will take time to bow before Jesus and worship Him as I worship the Father.

I need to be conscious of Jesus' presence as my Almighty Redeemer, who is able to save me from my sins, cleanse me, and empower me to do right. As my Redeemer, He saves me from sin in this life and prepares me to enjoy eternity with Him and all who love Him.

As I seek Jesus daily, I will come to love Him as the Mighty God and place all my confidence in Him as my Strength. I need to ask Jesus to give me a direct, definite, unceasing faith in His power at work in me. As I rely more upon Him to remake my soul, He will show me everything He can do to transform my life.

*Today's Date:*_____

Today's Requests:

Answers to Prayer and Thanksgivings:

The Seventh Step to Serenity

Remove Your Defects

35

I Know God Will Help Me

> *Now faith is being sure of what we hope for and certain of what we do not see.*
>
> —Hebrews 11:1

God will not remove all of my character defects all at once. He will usually remove them slowly and only one defect at a time. Their slow removal can encourage my steady spiritual growth and keep me relying daily on God for absolutely everything. Jesus trained His disciples to expect delay sometimes when they prayed. He encouraged them to keep on trusting in God and persevering in prayer until His mighty power brought them the answer they needed.

When the answers to my prayers do not come according to my timing, the promises I firmly trust can appear to be false. In the trial of "unanswered prayer," I need to wait on God with patience. Through patience in times of trial, God will purify and strengthen my faith. By faith, I need to grasp and hold the promises of God until I receive the fulfillment of all that God promises in His Word. God may seem slow to act, but I have found that He is always on time. God knows when everything is right for giving me the answer I seek. He can answer my prayers the most effectively for everyone according to His perfect timing; therefore, I pray for His perfect timing in every prayer.

God requires persevering prayer. Jesus taught that if an unfriendly, selfish neighbor would give someone what he needed when he kept asking, then God would give far more, because God is an unselfish, loving, Heavenly Father. When God delays in giving me what I need, He is teaching me to live with Him in undoubting faith and trust—to indeed become His friend, and not just want the things He has to give. God may delay in removing my shortcomings, but by His grace and through trusting prayer each day, He will eventually remove them all.

Jesus did not promise to heal my every physical disease, but He did promise to save me from my sins. As I go to Him each day, I need to tell Him specifically the character flaws that I want Him to remove, and then by faith begin thanking Him for their removal. As the Spirit of Jesus works in me, I will see myself growing in obedience, and gaining power over the temptations and compulsions that once had absolute power and control over me.

*Today's Date:*_____

Today's Requests:

Answers to Prayer and Thanksgivings:

Think of Others

36

Some Benefits of Making Amends

A new command I give you: Love one another. As I have loved you, so you must love one another.

—John 13:34

Jesus did not need to make amends to anyone for anything He ever did, for He never did anything to harm God or others. In some mysterious way, however, when He died on the cross, He made amends for me in ways that I could never do. I could spend the rest of my life trying to make everything right with God and others, and repair all the damage that I have ever done, but I would never be able to get completely right with God and others—or live in the present for the future.

Being willing to make amends to everyone is a part of my healing for spiritual and psychological reasons that only those who have done so can begin to understand. I found freedom from guilt, resentment, anger, and from blaming others for my mistakes. I began to take responsibility for my life in a more mature way. I found that my misdeeds no longer hung over my head and accused me of anything done (or not done) as they once did. I felt that peace within that I have heard so many others talk about having within them.

As I become more like Jesus, and begin to love others as He loves me, I become more willing to make amends wherever I can. I begin to pray for and seek ways to restore broken friendships and relationships. Where I have not yet found a way to make amends with some, I begin to pray for God to bless them. My prayers become more concerned for the welfare of others. I ask God about how I can make up with them or bless them, and not just further my own recovery and serenity.

Jesus' command insures me of His power to carry it out. If I ask Him, God will always give me the power to do His will. If I do not go to God in prayer first, God will sometimes let me fail in my own strength to teach me dependence on Him.

*Today's Date:*_____

Today's Requests:

Answers to Prayer and Thanksgivings:

Think of Others

37

Forgiving Helps Me Make Amends

> *And when you stand praying, if you hold anything against anyone, forgive him, so that your Father in heaven may forgive you your sins.*
>
> —Mark 11:25

I am tempted to rationalize, and resent people for what they did to me, rather than accept any responsibility for my own actions. These people are the very last I will think about with regard to making amends. Indeed, I may feel they need to make amends to me, and hold a grudge against them until they do.

Realizing how I feel about some who have offended me motivates me to think about how I can make amends to everyone I have offended. If I hold grudges against some who have hurt me, I need to ask God to help me to change. If I find it difficult to forgive someone who has not come first to make amends to me, I can help them and myself by going to them and seeking their forgiveness. I must begin. Eventually, I will forgive everyone who has hurt me. And, sometimes, others will begin to make amends to me.

If I refuse to forgive others, whether or not they have made amends to me; if I refuse to think about seeking their forgiveness by trying to undo any harm I may have done them, my attitude will interfere with my prayers and serenity. As I become more and more willing to do God's will in this matter, He will give me greater freedom in prayer. I will forgive others. As far as it is possible and proper, I will seek the forgiveness of any I have harmed.

Jesus' love in my heart motivates me to seek the happiness of others—especially those I have harmed in any way. My hurtful words or actions may be keeping some from coming to God, if they blame God for what I did. Making amends to them may be the answer to their prayers and restore their confidence in God. If I make amends with the love of Jesus shining forth from my heart, some may see the love of God for them and come to accept Him.

Jesus rescued me from my compulsive behaviors and unhealthy dependencies not just to make me happy. That was only the beginning for me. Jesus wants me to share His love in words and in the heavenly power of His love in my life.

*Today's Date:*_____

Today's Requests:

Answers to Prayer and Thanksgivings:

Think of Others

38

I Will Take Up My Cross

Anyone who does not take his cross and follow me is not worthy of me. Whoever finds his life will lose it, and whoever loses his life for my sake will find it.

—Matthew 10:38, 39

Every prayer step to serenity leads me to greater humility. Now I need to be willing to face the person I have wronged, confess my shortcomings to them, and offer to make things right if I can. This will be especially difficult if I believe they have also wronged me and are undeserving of my going to them to make amends. I need to pray for God to give me the willingness to complete this step to serenity and experience greater power in prayer.

As a believer in Jesus, with almost every step I take, He requires me to take up my cross and follow Him. Every step requires more of my self-life to die so God can live in and rule my life. When I pick up my cross to make amends to others, I die to self-pleasing and self-exaltation. God gives me additional inner peace, power and happiness. Each time I die to self, I find it easier to pray, because I am becoming more like my heavenly companion.

The cross is an instrument of execution: I need the death of my self-centeredness. Until I die to self-centeredness, I will not humble myself enough to make amends to those I may have harmed who do not suspect my shortcomings. I may not need to make amends to them directly. I may need to stay anonymous as I make amends. But right now, I need to pray for God to help me become willing to make amends. I know that after I prayerfully take this step to serenity that God will also give me the wisdom and the power to take the next one—one day at a time.

Today's Date:_____

Today's Requests:

Answers to Prayer and Thanksgivings:

Think of Others

39

Willing to Give Up Everything

In the same way, any of you who does not give up everything he has cannot be my disciple.

—Luke 14:33

Jesus does not require me to take a vow of poverty and live off others to be His disciple. Indeed, many who have come to know Jesus, or who have walked the prayer steps, have overcome poverty and the need to depend on others instead of on God.

Jesus does not want me to consider my possessions as my own, but as gifts from God to use to bless others as well as myself. I am not to be self-centered or selfish when I see the needs of others, but ask God how or if I can help them.

By following the Lord daily, He will first lead me to become willing to make amends to those I have wronged. This may require giving back something I have stolen, or returning money I have acquired by dishonest or unethical means. If I have given all that I am and possess to God, it will be easier for me to accept the idea of making restitution wherever God shows me the need. He will use what I have already given Him to meet the needs of others.

Jesus Christ claims all from me, and then He begins to meet my every need, giving a hundred times more than I give up. This may not always mean material blessings, but it does mean spiritual satisfaction and serenity. As I think about what I have had to give up with each serenity step, I thank God for the many blessings each renunciation of my selfishness has brought others and me. I know that through Jesus Christ my spiritual life will get better and better (and often He will give me the material blessings I need).

As I learn what it means to believe Christ is my life, I will count all things as loss for the excellence of knowing Jesus Christ as my Lord. In the path of following and loving Him, I am willing to sacrifice all to make room in my life for the One who is more than every thing that exists in this world, for He created everything.

*Today's Date:*_____

Today's Requests:

Answers to Prayer and Thanksgivings:

The Eighth Step to Serenity

Think of Others

40

Willing to Face What I Lack

> *Jesus looked at him and loved him. "One thing you lack," he said. "Go, sell everything you have and give to the poor, and you will have treasure in heaven. Then come, follow me."*
>
> —Mark 10:21

If my spiritual development seems to be slowing or my serenity seems to be slipping away, perhaps I am experiencing difficulty in doing all that following Jesus means In the depth of my heart, I need to become *willing* to make amends—that is my next step. I need to look honestly at what that demands of me. Am I now *willing* to sacrifice my prestige, power, or position to make everything right with others, especially if this may come at great personal cost? I may not have hit bottom before seeking spiritual life and healing, so becoming *willing* to make amends and then *making* amends may be particularly difficult for me. Yet, if I do not keep walking in these prayer steps, I could fall back into destructive habits.

In my own strength, I cannot complete any of these prayer steps to serenity. Thank God, the Holy Spirit will give me the strength I need to go on. Jesus promised, "All things are possible with God" (Mark 10:27). Trying to follow Jesus each day reveals to me exactly how much I need Jesus in my spiritual life. Christ's Spirit in me will help me become willing to sacrifice myself, or my possessions, to restore in some way what I have destroyed.

When Peter confessed Jesus as Lord, Jesus declared that he could only do that by divine teaching and the power of God. Only by divine power will I be able to accept what the prayer steps offer me and walk in them. I need to pray daily for God to give me the willingness to do whatever He wants, and the wisdom to see what He requires. No one has ever naturally become willing to make amends, or made amends, without the help of God and the divine leading to seek out only those He wants them to help.

Some have sought to walk the walk and follow Christ without seeking God's power through prayer, and they have failed. Some have felt that serenity was beyond their reach and have given up. They failed to realize that they needed Jesus Christ as their Higher Power to enable them to do all that God requires to receive His many blessings each day.

*Today's Date:*_____

Today's Requests:

Answers to Prayer and Thanksgivings:

Right Your Wrongs

41

I Will Avoid Making Excuses

Do everything without complaining or arguing, so that you may become blameless and pure, children of God without fault in a crooked and depraved generation, in which you shine like stars in the universe.

—Philippians 2:14, 15

As my learning increases from studying and practicing these prayer steps to serenity, I may be tempted to put my limited judgment over God's infinite wisdom. I may begin to think that I do not need to make amends to others—that my *being willing* to make amends is enough. I can imagine all sorts of reasons to avoid this step and move on. I might think that my spiritual awakening has gone so well that I can stop working the steps now and everything will still be okay. If I rely on myself alone to move on in the prayer steps, instead of on my Lord and Savior, I will not complete the prayer steps to serenity, and not finishing what I have begun will hinder my healing and rob me of God's promised peace.

I need to be careful and not rationalize that I would only hurt others by trying to make amends. This may simply be my way of avoiding something I anticipate will make me uncomfortable or increase my pain. Have I really *become willing* to make amends? And have I become willing to make amends *to everyone*?

The question may be one of pride in human wisdom and achievement. I need to remind myself again and again that humility is the key to my progress. With humility, I need to go to God in prayer and confess my absolute dependence on Him for taking this next step. I need the Holy Spirit to teach me why making amends is so important, to give me the power to complete it, and to show me exactly the person or people I must make amends to help.

In this prayer step, I will learn to rely on God day by day and moment by moment. I will pray without ceasing for the right attitude, actions and words as I make amends. I will pray that my making of amends will bless the person I speak with, and that the Holy Spirit will have prepared their hearts to hear my confession and willingness to repair what I have broken. Lord Jesus, I am depending on you to lead the way.

*Today's Date:*_____

Today's Requests:

Answers to Prayer and Thanksgivings:

Right Your Wrongs

42

The Holy Spirit Will Help Me

He will bring glory to me by taking from what is mine and making it known to you.

—John 16:14

I can receive the gift of the Holy Spirit through faith in Jesus Christ. When I follow Jesus Christ, the Spirit flows like a river within me. The Spirit flows from the Lord Jesus. The Spirit reveals and imparts Him to me. Jesus Christ sent the Holy Spirit from heaven so the Holy Spirit could glorify Jesus in the heart of every believer, and be revealed through the life of His followers.

The fullness of God dwelt in Jesus Christ in order for Christ, as the life of God, to dwell in His followers. All the life and love, which the Spirit imparts, is in Christ Jesus. My whole spiritual life consists in union with Him. Each new day, I need to praise God that Jesus lives in me, and ask

Him to make His presence an abiding reality in my life. I need to rely upon the unseen working of the Holy Spirit in my heart.

With Jesus Christ living in me, I can impart something of His divine life and love to others as I make amends. Some will see the love of Christ shinning forth in me. I will glorify God as people see that my making amends comes from the spiritual renewal Jesus Christ makes in my life.

Some people will understand that my attempts to make things right with them indicate the progress I am making in this journey toward serenity. These people will receive me with an open and forgiving heart. If they can also see that my making amends comes from the work of God in me, they will glorify God, and the Holy Spirit will continue keeping me humble when I do right.

In the life and words of His disciples, antagonistic leaders recognized that His followers had been with Jesus Christ. As I spend daily time with Christ in prayer and meditation upon the Scriptures, the Holy Spirit will work in me so those I fear most may be able see God living and working in me.

*Today's Date:*_____

Today's Requests:

Answers to Prayer and Thanksgivings:

Right Your Wrongs

43

When Christ is My Life

> *When Christ, who is your life, appears, then you also will appear with him in glory.*
>
> —Colossians 3:4

Many people believe that Jesus died on the cross for them and now lives in heaven. However, few people believe and live as though Jesus Christ lives within them. The powerlessness of many is mainly due to this narrow view. Do I really believe that the Almighty Lord dwells within me? Do I really believe that His Presence in me is the only source of true serenity?

Believing that Jesus lives in me, and that Christ is my hope for glory, will free me to make amends without fearing the consequences. Through daily prayer, Christ will give me the direction and power to make amends in the best way possible. I will not simply say, "Jesus died for me, so my sins are forgiven. I do not need to do any more," and then ignore making things right with those I have harmed. No. I will say, "Jesus died for me and now lives in me to help me overcome my sins and to help me right the wrongs I have caused others and myself. By His power, I will remedy the harm I have caused. Others may see Him alive and working in me; therefore, others may seek Him and the joy I have found through trusting Him."

I need to know, experience, and testify to the truth that Christ lives in me. I cannot use my newly found faith as an excuse for not righting wrongs wherever I can. Jesus lives in me so I can pray to know the right and have the power to do it.

As others receive my offer to restore what I have destroyed, they may see that these efforts flow from my desire to live wholly for God in Christ Jesus. Perhaps I can tell them that my efforts to make things right with them come from my desire to have an abiding fellowship with Christ Jesus and do His will at all times and in everything. Perhaps they too will want and seek this joyous relationship with God through Jesus that brings me such happiness and serenity.

Some may ask why I am trying to do what they themselves know they need to do. This will give me an opportunity to say that Christ lives in me, and I now want to live for Him. Taking this prayer step and making amends may give me the opportunity to help others find the spiritual healing and strength they need.

*Today's Date:*_____

Today's Requests:

Answers to Prayer and Thanksgivings:

Right Your Wrongs

44

Prayer Helps in Making Amends

> *Pray in the Spirit on all occasions with all kinds of prayers and requests. With this in mind, be alert and always keep on praying for all the saints.*
> —Ephesians 6:18

I will not be alone and powerless to make amends when others pray for me as I reach out to those I have wronged. I can ask those close to me, who believe in the power of prayer, to prepare the persons I must speak to and prepare me to say and do the right things with the right timing. In the prayer steps to serenity, we do not need to make amends all alone—we can give prayer support to one another.

Thank God for the wonder of His grace: He tells us that we can pray down heavenly gifts to bless one another. My making the effort to make amends may be the most difficult and responsible action I have ever taken. With God going with me and preparing the way, with God granting me spiritual success within as I make the attempt to make amends, I know that He will give me the power to do whatever else the prayer steps require. I do pray today that the serenity I have come to know from practicing these prayer steps will be with me as I make amends to those I have hurt.

If I fail to pray for others as they make amends, they may suffer from my neglect. If I say I will pray for them, perhaps I need to pray right then, and pray with them for the success of their efforts. In working through the prayer steps, I am not alone.

The prayer steps to serenity require that I make amends where possible, and where it will not hurt others. God will show me how to avoid hurting others: either by not making amends to them or by not making amends to them in the wrong way. My efforts to make amends will show me how much I need to depend on God for everything.

If I cannot make amends personally, I can pray for God to make amends for me. God can restore to others what I cannot restore myself. God can bless those I have hurt, and give them happiness where I am powerless. However, I cannot allow prayer to be the substitute for whatever God wants me to do in personal action.

*Today's Date:*_____

Today's Requests:

Answers to Prayer and Thanksgivings:

The Ninth Step to Serenity

Right Your Wrongs

45

I Will Not Give Up

Jesus told his disciples . . . that they should always pray and not give up.
—Luke 18:1

One of the greatest drawbacks in praying for God's guidance in making amends is the long delay I will sometimes experience in receiving His leading for specific people. This should not surprise me when I remember that God is preparing me to make amends and others to receive my efforts. I must not rush ahead of God to complete this step, and God may want me to keep coming back to work this step as I grow spiritually and He makes me ready over time. I will not fail to move to the next step just because God is not ready for me to reach out *to everyone* on my list at this time.

God may have good reasons for delaying His answers to my prayers. My desire to make amends will grow deeper and stronger as I pray daily for the ones I need to reach out to and bless with my amends. My love for them will grow as God's Spirit leads me in prayer. My prayers for them will become more effective. In God's timing, others will see God's love for them in my love for them. They will see God's love for them through the actions I take in the power of His Spirit.

God has put me in His school of prayer. When He delays in answering my prayers, His delays teach me to keep praying and not give up. As I persevere in prayer, God strengthens my faith. I need to believe that God has a great blessing for others and me from delayed answers. Experience teaches me that His delayed answers are always the best answers for everyone.

Above all, God wants to draw me into a closer fellowship with himself. When God delays His answers, I learn that nearness to God and love of God are more important than receiving the answers to my petitions—so I continue in prayer.

I need to remember the blessing Jacob received when God delayed in answering him. He eventually saw God face to face, and as a prince he had power with God and prevailed (see Genesis 32:28-30).

I must not become impatient or discouraged when God's answers do not come according to my time schedule, but continue in prayer. I can ask myself if my prayer is according to the will and Word of God. I can ask myself if my prayer is in the right spirit and in the name of Jesus Christ. I can ask myself if I have really forgiven others, and especially the person I need to make amends to in taking this prayer step. If I persevere in prayer, God will teach me what I need to do to secure His answer.

*Today's Date:*_____

Today's Requests:

Answers to Prayer and Thanksgivings:

Practice Doing Right

46

Reasons for Lack of Prayer

Do not think of yourself more highly than you ought, but rather think of yourself with sober judgment, in accordance with the measure of faith God has given you.

—Romans 12:3

I must not consider my circumstances a good excuse for my lack of prayer. God's Word tells me to look in my heart for the real reasons. Deep inside, I may sometimes feel hostility toward God and do not want to be with Him. Sometimes I may refuse to yield entirely to the Holy Spirit's leading. Sometimes I am still afraid to let go and let God take total control of my life. When I do this, before I realize it, my emotions have taken control of me.

I need to take a personal inventory each day, and check for any indications that I may have been stepping backwards:

- Have I been too hasty in my words and actions?
- Has anger been arising unexpectedly within me?
- Do I sense a lack of love for God and others?
- Do I derive too much pleasure in eating and drinking?
- Has my conscience been accusing me of misbehavior?
- Have I been seeking my own will and honor?
- Have I been putting too much confidence in my own power?
- Have I thought I could trust in my wisdom alone?

I can trace the reasons for a lack of quiet time, prayer, and serenity if I answer any of these questions with a "yes."

I am to live in the Spirit, but sometimes I refuse to walk in the Spirit. When this happens, my feelings become my lord and I become a willing slave to my emotions. When I recognize any of the above symptoms, I must ask God to forgive me, free me from these defects, and once again fill me with His love. By His grace, God will help me come to Him honestly, and give me the power to pray and joyfully to seek His fellowship each day.

*Today's Date:*_____

Today's Requests:

Answers to Prayer and Thanksgivings:

Practice Doing Right

47

Overcoming Satan

For our struggle is not against flesh and blood, but against the rulers, against the authorities, against the powers of this dark world and against the spiritual forces of evil in the heavenly realms.

—Ephesians 6:12

I must never forget that Satan will always be my enemy. He wants to destroy my life, and he will use every weapon at his disposal. Therefore, I thank God that through the weapon of prayer, Satan can be defeated. No wonder Satan will do his best to take this weapon from my hands or try to keep me from my quiet times alone with God.

Satan will tempt me to postpone or shorten my time in prayer. He will influence my thoughts to wander and bring distractions into my mind. He will try to sway me toward unbelief and hopelessness. He will inflame my emotions and turn me toward putting myself first above all others.

Nevertheless, I can overcome Satan, regain serenity, and return to happiness when I hold fast and keep using my weapon of prayer against all obstacles. When our Lord Jesus was in Gethsemane, as Satan attacked more viciously, He prayed ever more fervently. I can do the same. Jesus prayed, and did not cease until He rose victorious. I can follow His example, and the Holy Spirit will give me the will and strength to do so.

Without daily prayer, meditation, and self-examination in my quiet times, Satan can quickly gain a foothold in my life. I must pray; for without prayer, the helmet of salvation, the shield of faith and the sword of the Spirit (which is God's Word), will have no power to defend me and defeat my spiritual foes (see Ephesians 6:13-18). All depends on God and His promises, and persevering prayer enables Him to fulfill these quickly. May God be gracious, and teach me to believe in Him and the power of daily prayer.

*Today's Date:*_____

Today's Requests:

Answers to Prayer and Thanksgivings:

Practice Doing Right

48

I Train with a Goal

Everyone who competes in the games goes into strict training. Therefore I do not run like a man running aimlessly.

—1 Corinthians 9:26, 27

By walking the prayer steps to serenity, I am bringing order into my life. Sometimes, I have slipped back into old attitudes and behaviors, and I have said and done things that have hurt others and me. When this has happened, I have promptly admitted my wrongs and made amends where necessary; if I have not, the loss of my serenity has sometimes led me to worse thoughts, words, actions, and prayerlessness. When I am tempted to succumb to my cravings or weaknesses, I have learned that I can pray "The Serenity Prayer": "God grant me the serenity to accept the things I cannot change, the courage to change the things I can, and the wisdom to know the difference." I try to focus my prayers on wisdom, courage, and God's help and guidance when I make decisions.

I need to remember I am in strict training for a spiritual goal. I need to give up everything that might be attractive but harmful to my spiritual growth and progress. Each day, when I take a new personal inventory of my moral condition, I need to ask myself what things I could have omitted or added that day as a part of my training. This can be a vitally important part of my daily quiet time.

Jesus wants me to have an undivided heart. He does not want me to strive for earthly prizes and glory as though these were more important than the heavenly gifts. Have I been spending more time preparing myself for earthly success and accolades than I have for enjoying the eternal rewards? Do I have a divided heart? On the other hand, have I found that I swing back and forth between God and the world too often and for the wrong reasons?

The Apostle Paul would not let anything deter him from pressing toward the mark for the prize. No self-pleasing in eating and drinking, no comfort or ease kept him for a moment from showing the spirit of the cross in his daily life. No thought of self kept him from sacrificing his all for his Master. Likewise, the cross needs to be the goal of my life too. God must be first in my life.

I need to pray: "O God, give me the spirit of the cross through the power of the Holy Spirit. When the death of Christ works in me, I will make His life known to others through me. Jesus humbled himself and became obedient unto death on the cross. Lord Jesus, please give me this attitude, and show me daily what I need to do in order to pick up my cross and follow you."

*Today's Date:*_____

Today's Requests:

Answers to Prayer and Thanksgivings:

The Tenth Step to Serenity

Practice Doing Right

49

Abiding in Christ

We always carry around in our body the death of Jesus, so that the life of Jesus may also be revealed in our body.

—2 Corinthians 4:10, 12

As I pray through these steps and continue my recovery, I see new heights to reach. Things I never thought of as wrong before now seem horrible. As the Holy Spirit works within me, He shows me things to remove that are incompatible with His full presence in my life. Yet, most importantly, He wants me to be Christ-centered instead of me-centered.

As I spend more time in prayer, I am learning the meaning of abiding in Christ. At first, this meant to me simply affirming His presence with me each day. Now, I am learning that it also means abiding in the crucified Christ. Once, I thought I only had to affirm once, and for all time, "I am crucified with Christ." Now, I see that I am to abide daily in the fellowship of His death by taking the form of a servant, a servant who seeks to bless God and others.

Jesus humbled himself and became obedient unto death—this mind of Christ needs to be the spirit that marks my daily life. However, I need to pray, that as I become more and more like Christ in His death, that I do not continue to sustain or return to destructive co-dependent relationships. The Holy Spirit will give me wisdom as I pray for His daily light in applying the Scriptures.

Jesus calls me to bear about in my body His dying for others and me. I am to live for the welfare of others. As I suffer with Christ, the crucified Lord can work out His life through me to help others. Am I doing this each day? Am I willing to do this? Am I willing for my self-centeredness to die through my quiet times with God, so a new Christ-centeredness will live? Am I willing to live so others can see Jesus alive in me? I have discovered the joy of this sacrifice, and this moves me to stay true to Him.

*Today's Date:*_____

Today's Requests:

Answers to Prayer and Thanksgivings:

Practice Doing Right

50

I Died on Christ's Cross

> *Christ himself bore our sins in his body on the tree, so that we might die to sins and live for righteousness; by his wounds you have been healed.*
> —1 Peter 2:24

If I do not keep my eyes on Jesus as I review my life each day, I can become discouraged and think there is no hope for me. The things I hate doing, I seem to do repeatedly. I do not know how God can forgive me unless I remember that Jesus bore my sins in His body on the cross. I will spend a part of my quiet time looking to Jesus as I see Him hanging on the cross for me.

I will not be able to live unto righteousness unless I know that I have died to sin. The Holy Spirit needs to make my death to sin in Christ such a reality that I know myself to be forever free from its power. In addition, I need to yield myself completely to God, asking Him to forgive me and make me an instrument of righteousness, a true joy to God and others. I need to consider myself both dead to sin and alive to Jesus Christ.

It has not been easy for me to understand or experience what it means to die to sin and live to righteousness, but dying with Christ on His cross remains the key to victory over sin and temptation. By God's grace through faith, I actually shared with Christ in His death. I need to understand that winning the victory will require self-sacrifice and earnest prayer. It will cost me a whole-hearted surrender to God and His will. It will require abiding and unceasing fellowship with the crucified Christ.

If these things have not been my heart's desire, am I willing to recognize these as shortcomings? Do I actually prefer to live on the level of law and morality, just trying to do what I think I ought to do, instead of stepping up to the heights of a new spirituality of love and devotion? Will I resolve to love God with all my heart? Will I choose to make the effort to love and serve others? Or will I be satisfied with a low view of daily living and miss all the joy and peace that God wants to give me?

As I pray through these prayer steps, resolving to live in full obedience to God, the Holy Spirit will teach me the secret of dying with Christ, of dying to selfishness, of living fully in and for God.

*Today's Date:*_____

Today's Requests:

Answers to Prayer and Thanksgivings:

Pray to God

51

True Prayer Leads to True Fellowship

> *To them God has chosen to make known among the Gentiles the glorious riches of this mystery, which is Christ in you, the hope of glory.*
>
> —Colossians 1:27

True prayer gives me contact with God. As I seek the holiness of God by persistent prayer, God covers my sinfulness with His holiness. As I get to know God better, my understanding of His greatness and power makes me more humble and holy.

True prayer leads me to see that I can have fellowship with God only if I choose the road of humility, just as Christ humbled himself. When Jesus Christ becomes my daily example and guide in prayer, I truly live in Christ, just as Christ lives in the Father.

Above everything, true prayer consists in fellowship with God, with God's bringing me under the power of His holiness and love. This fellowship comes from the daily quiet times I enjoy. Through daily contact with God, He possesses me and stamps my entire personality with the lowliness and loveliness of His Son. In friendship with my Redeemer, I find the secret of true love for God and others. As my Friend, Jesus will guide me and direct me in my prayers and in all of my other relationships.

In Jesus Christ, I draw near to God. I have died with Christ, so Christ can reign in my life. By the power of the Holy Spirit, I need to affirm with assurance, "Christ lives in me." As I affirm this truth with absolute trust in His word, others will see Christ living in me too.

Praying to the Father in the name of Jesus causes me to experience new joys and gives me greater power in prayer. I pray that God will strengthen me, and encourage me to believe in the certain victory He will bring. Trust in Him will give me the daily serenity I seek. Through true prayer, I can receive blessings that are greater than I could imagine. God will do this for all who love Him, so I pray for Him to keep my love constant and sincere.

I have found that daily victory in prayer does not come immediately or all at one time. God's fatherly patience continues toward me: He bears with His children. I rejoice in the promises I find throughout God's Word in my quiet time. In addition, as my faith grows stronger through prayer, I will persevere to the end and enjoy victory over my self-centeredness.

*Today's Date:*_____

Today's Requests:

Answers to Prayer and Thanksgivings:

Pray to God

52

God Will Not Forsake Me

Those who know your name will trust in you, for you, LORD, have never forsaken those who seek you.

—Psalm 9:10

When I pray for more of the Holy Spirit to help me in my weakness and draw me closer to God, I need to remember that the Holy Spirit wants more of me too. The Spirit of God wants to possess me entirely. Just as my soul indwells my body, so my body can serve me, the Holy Spirit wants to indwell my body and soul fully, so I can serve God. God wants His dwelling entirely under His control.

Until I have learned to trust God fully, I will not be ready to continue in the prayer steps to serenity and make spiritual progress. As God demonstrates His love and faithfulness to me daily, He will overcome my fear of giving Him total control of my life. Such total commitment will result supernaturally, as I go to God in prayer and surrender each day to His care.

As I work through the prayer steps with reliance on God, the Holy Spirit will gently lead me to make entirely new and deeper consecrations to God. The Spirit will inspire me to seek more and more of God in my personal experience. The Holy Spirit will show me how Jesus Christ will deliver me from all my character defects. Jesus Christ, the Almighty Deliverer, will come near to defend me and draw me nearer to God. The Holy Spirit will lead me in my prayers for deliverance until I find the victory.

The Spirit of God will help me forget myself and seek more of God in prayer. Eventually, He will make me willing to put my needs aside, so He can train me to intercede for others, especially those who need deliverance from the same afflictions and weakness I have suffered. The Holy Spirit will make me willing to trust God to carry out His plans for my life and His plans for those I love and care for. He will never leave me or forsake me in trouble.

*Today's Date:*_____

Today's Requests:

Answers to Prayer and Thanksgivings:

Pray to God

53

I Am Crucified to Overcome

> *I have been crucified with Christ and I no longer live, but Christ lives in me. The life I live in the body, I live by faith in the Son of God, who loved me and gave himself for me.*
>
> —Galatians 2:20

As I have tried to work the prayer steps to serenity in the light of the Scriptures, I have found the lesson of the cross the most difficult to learn. Jesus said, "Take my yoke upon you and learn from me, for I am gentle and humble in heart, and you will find rest for your souls. For my yoke is easy and my burden is light" (Matthew 11:29, 30). Through the love of Christ on the cross, He draws me to Him, and I receive His promise to help me bear my cross with perfect serenity each day.

Love makes everything easy. His love for me, and my love for Him and others, flows as His Spirit moves in my heart with a love and peace beyond human understanding. I need to meditate day and night on His love for me as He died on the cross, until the Holy Spirit gives me personal assurance of His love and daily help in all my struggles. I must not forsake a daily quiet time with God.

I need the Holy Spirit to breathe into my heart daily "you are a child of God" and give me joy unspeakable. When I remember that the blood of Jesus washed away my sins, I have proof that God will never reject me—His child. Through the power of Jesus' shed blood, I become pleasing to God in my thoughts and actions.

As I seek to know God's will daily, asking Him for the power I need to carry it out, I also need to see myself as a ruler and intercessor (as king and priest) in Jesus' name. God will strengthen me through His power, so I can conquer my character defects, overcome my temptations, and receive His courage and joy.

God will also encourage me to intercede for others each day as I seek His will for my life that day. Through my prayers, others will more easily discover God's will for their lives. They will yield their lives to His love and grace.

*Today's Date:*_____

Today's Requests:

Answers to Prayer and Thanksgivings:

Pray to God

54

Reasons for Effective Prayer

Therefore, confess your sins to each other and pray for each other so that you may be healed. The prayer of a righteous man is powerful and effective.

—James 5:16

Prayer avails much with God, and the history of His people proves it. Prayer is the one great power I can exercise to secure the working of God's almighty power in my life and in the world.

The prayer of a righteous person avails much. The Scriptures teach that a believer's righteousness is in Christ: not simply as a garment covering the person, but as an indwelling life-power in a person made new by Christ.

As I seek God, God's will for my life, and God's power to obey day by day, I will be what the Scriptures call "an instrument of righteousness"

(Romans 6:13). My true joy and effectiveness in prayer will depend on my relying daily on the righteousness of Christ working in me. As I surrender to God, I will be more useful each day. As I spend time quietly with God in prayer and Scripture study, He will show me what to do and who to reach out to help. His Spirit will give me the wisdom to do everything His way and in His perfect timing. His Spirit will prepare others to receive the good things that I intend to do for them from a heart of love.

On the night before He died, Jesus gave His wonderful prayer promises to those who obey: "If you love me, you will obey what I command. And I will ask the Father, and he will give you another Counselor to be with you forever—the Spirit of truth" (John 14:15-17). "If you remain in me and my words remain in you, ask whatever you wish, and it will be given you. If you obey my commands, you will remain in my love, just as I have obeyed my Father's commands and remain in his love" (John 15:7 & 10). If I practice Jesus' precious promises in His name, my prayers will be powerful and effective.

Only when a righteous person rouses his whole being to take hold of God will prayer avail much. The effective, fervent prayers of righteous people effect great things. Wherever two or three righteous people agree, Jesus has promised to answer prayers in His name. I need to meditate on how much Christ could do if hundreds of those who are truly righteous in Christ also united in prayer. I can pray for this unity in Christ among His people, and that God will use me to bring about this unity in Christ wherever biblical.

As I maintain my quiet times, may I see the importance of living my life in Christ before and after I pray in Christ. If my prayers are not effective, maybe I need to pray through some of the earlier prayer steps once again.

*Today's Date:*_____

Today's Requests:

Answers to Prayer and Thanksgivings:

Pray to God

55

Reasons for Daily Prayer

Give us each day our daily bread.

—Luke 11:3

Once, I was afraid to pledge that I would pray to God each day or commit myself to a daily quiet time in meditation on the word of God. I thought making such a demand upon myself and the daily commitment was altogether beyond me. Then, I discovered that I did pray each day for daily bread, and I found myself wanting to spend more time with God.

Surely, if I have once yielded my whole heart to God's love and service, I should count it a privilege to take advantage of God's invitation to come into His presence and tell Him my every need and the great needs of others each day. Can I believe that He has truly humbled himself to invite me to spend time with Him? Can I believe that the great Creator of the universe values me so much as to want to spend time with me? Yes. The Bible tells me so, and His love for me in my heart confirms the truth of His word.

Do I still desire to live wholly for God? Jesus Christ gave himself for me, and His love now watches over me and works in me daily without ceasing. Surely, I will welcome the opportunity that practicing these prayer steps gives me to prove day by day that I am devoting my heart's strength to the interests of God's kingdom. Surely, I will rejoice in the honor of Jesus asking me to bring down God's blessings upon others through daily prayer and meditation.

The Bible reminds me to call out to God each day for His power. My needs and the needs of others are far beyond my ability to meet without the promise of God's power. As I praise God for what His power has done for others and me, I am amazed at what He has enabled us to carry out.

I need to pray for God to lead others of like mind to me. We can pray and work together to accomplish His will. I have found great freedom and wonderful healing as I have prayed with others who have problems similar to mine. I will find great power, and be more effective in prayer, as God unites me with those who know Him as I do—through Jesus Christ. Without doubt, this must be a part of my seeking God's will for my life, and of my receiving serenity through humble submission to God in the service of others.

*Today's Date:*_____

Today's Requests:

Answers to Prayer and Thanksgivings:

Seek to Serve

56

The Power of Intercession

> *We are therefore Christ's ambassadors, as though God were making his appeal through us. We implore you on Christ's behalf: Be reconciled to God.*
> —2 Corinthians 5:20

Let me consecrate myself to interceding more for others. The Apostle Paul wrote of praying for those he had not even met. Though he was personally subject to the limitations of time and space, in the Spirit, he had power in the name of Jesus Christ to pray for a blessing on those who had not heard of the Savior. If he could not reach them himself, he prayed for others to help them.

Let me pray each day for those who need to find God and deliverance, whether I know them personally or not. I can pray for the opportunity to tell them about God and the prayer steps to serenity that will free them from their bondage to negative thinking and injurious actions. I can pray for God to give me just the right words to share with every needy person He brings across my path, whether inside or outside my circle of family and friends.

Paul lived a heavenly life of love and amazing power in prayer. If I start living a life of prayer, God will give me this same power. I need to pray for greater boldness and daring to reach up to heaven in the mighty name of Jesus Christ in order to bring down a blessing on those who need God. Many need freedom from despair, discouragement, fear, pride and other problems.

Imagine what would happen if more believers, say twice as many as before, could be brought by God's grace to pray for others with twofold faith and joy. A gentle power would come down in our prayer meetings, if people would spend more time in prayer before and during our times together. Each one would experience and share the serenity we seek. If I prayed more (privately and with others), it would make a wonderful difference in the numbers of people I could help.

*Today's Date:*_____

Today's Requests:

Answers to Prayer and Thanksgivings:

Seek to Serve

57

God Calls Me to Tell Others

> *You will receive power when the Holy Spirit comes on you; and you will be my witnesses in Jerusalem, and in all Judea and Samaria, and to the ends of the earth.*
>
> —Acts 1:8

Since I have worked through the prayer steps and have come to know my Savior more personally through prayer, I am now ready to point others to the person and program that can work for them. Jesus called His servants to witness for Him, to testify to His wonderful love and power to redeem, to tell others about His continual abiding presence and wonderful ability to work miracles in their lives. Indeed, my spiritual awakening and improvement one day at a time qualifies as a miracle, especially when I look back and see what God has done through prayer. To witness, I simply need to tell what God and these prayer steps have done for me.

Witnessing is the only outward weapon the Great King allows His redeemed ones to use. Without claiming special authority or power, without worldly wisdom or eloquent speech, without social status or privilege, I need to witness by my life and actions and be a living proof and witness of what Jesus can do. In this way, I do not point with pride to myself, but humbly to Jesus as my Higher Power.

Not by my words only, but by my transformed life, the Spirit will bring others to the feet of Jesus for salvation here and hereafter. When the Holy Spirit filled the first disciples, they began to speak of the mighty things Jesus had done. I need to pray for the same Spirit to help others find the open secret that I have discovered through my spiritual awakening.

In the power of the Spirit, the disciples helped others in the name of Jesus. Filled with the life and love of Jesus, they spoke of what Jesus had done for them, and this gave the good news power to help others. Here we have the secret of a flourishing spiritual fellowship—every believer bearing witness for Jesus and telling what He does for people.

*Today's Date:*_____

Today's Requests:

Answers to Prayer and Thanksgivings:

Seek to Serve

58

What May Set Me Apart

When the Counselor comes, whom I will send to you from the Father, the Spirit of truth who goes out from the Father, he will testify about me. And you also must testify, for you have been with me from the beginning.
—John 15:26, 27

Some have found help and sanity from sources other than the ones that helped me. Some view their Higher Power differently from me. I have learned not to proudly separate myself from them, or look down upon them, but thank God for them, and praise God for what He is doing in their lives thus far. God promises that all those who seek Him with all their hearts will find Him. I will pray for people to seek and find, and for myself too, to know God more fully in Jesus Christ and the Scriptures.

In working the prayer steps, I will tell others what God and Christ have done for me, and then I will let go and let God work. My prayers for wisdom and courage to speak will help me, but my prayers for those I tell about God and the prayer steps will help even more—I can pray for others when I cannot be with them, and the Holy Spirit can touch their hearts and minds with the truth. The Holy Spirit can fill them with God's love and lead them to those who will love them into believing and trusting in God.

What may separate me from others in my fellowship is the great truth that the Lord Jesus saved me and helped me with my recovery and spiritual progress. I will be saying that my spiritual awakening involved a new relationship with Jesus Christ. My talking about Jesus Christ and the power of prayer will be similar to the first disciples: they ceased not in every house to teach and to preach Jesus Christ. My Higher Power is Jesus. I am not ashamed to say so, even though my loyalty to Him may set me apart from others. If this happens, I will pray that others see the sweet, loving Spirit of Jesus in me and not the condemning arrogance or judgmental attitude they have sometimes seen in others.

God cleansed me to serve Him. Through prayer steps to serenity, when I was powerless, God restored me to sanity. Today, I find my life is creative, joyful, peaceful and full of God's love. I have an everlasting hope that I will see the Lord of glory. God taught me how to pray, and gave me His Spirit to teach me the Scriptures. God gave me a spiritual fellowship and a message to share. I have much, and even much more, for which to thank God in my quiet time today.

*Today's Date:*_____

Today's Requests:

Answers to Prayer and Thanksgivings:

Seek to Serve

59

My Personal Testimony

After they prayed, the place where they were meeting was shaken. And they were all filled with the Holy Spirit and spoke the word of God boldly. All the believers were one in heart and mind. No one claimed that any of his possessions was his own, but they shared everything they had.

—Acts 4:31, 32

I must base what I share with others about my healing and serenity on my personal experience with God, prayer, and the prayer steps I am taking. I can show others the Jesus of the Bible, but showing them Jesus in my life may be more effective in their lives at first. By the grace of God, my recovery and restoration to sanity, one day at a time, will show what Jesus can do and not what I have done. Above all, I need to stay personal. Those who need to take the journey I have taken have heard enough theories. They need to see what works and the One who works.

The Holy Spirit will show what Jesus and following in His steps can do as people look into my heart. If I rely on Jesus and ask Him to live His life daily through me, they may see the loving work of God in my life. I need to pray for the Holy Spirit to build me up, so I can walk in such fellowship with Jesus Christ that He can reveal himself through me. Only the Holy Spirit can lead me, and others, to understand the indispensable secrets of spiritual health. One secret is a life of prayer and daily fellowship with God. Another secret is a childlike love for God and true consecration to the Father and the Son in the power of the Holy Spirit.

I cannot fake a true spiritual awakening for others will see through me to the discredit of Jesus and the journey I have taken. I cannot allow myself to fall back into kidding myself by faking some spiritual trip. I need to pray that the spiritual truths I read about or discover (which I do not fully understand yet), will still be revealed to me personally by the Holy Spirit in some small way each day—for Christ's sake, for my sake, and for the sake of others.

*Today's Date:*_____

Today's Requests:

Answers to Prayer and Thanksgivings:

Seek to Serve

60
My Future Work Carrying the Message

"Come, follow me," Jesus said, "and I will make you fishers of men."
—Matthew 4:9

The Lord Jesus now expects me to help others find fellowship with Him. Since I have found a Higher Power and prayer steps that work, since God's love now fills my heart and motivates me, I can carry the message to others more effectively. A part of my continuing spiritual growth will depend on whether or not I remain God-centered and seek to share my testimony with others. I cannot allow myself to slip back into the self-absorption and self-centeredness that once destroyed my life and happiness.

I have discovered why prayer works. The Holy Spirit inspired His disciples to see the pattern of Jesus' prayer life and teachings; then, they followed Him in His prayer life and teachings. They wanted Jesus to pray in them and for them. Finally, in the Scriptures, they recorded what they saw, experienced, and learned about Jesus and the power of prayer. We now know that prayer works for all who follow Jesus and His teachings. The prayer steps teach those in recovery what God's Word teaches all Christians about their duty—the duty to pray for and help others in the name of Jesus and for His sake in the power of the Holy Spirit.

When I keep my heart right with God, I have freedom in definite, believing prayer and may expect God to bless my outreach to others. Having worked through the prayer steps, I understand the message so well that I can carry the message to others, but I need to remember to rely daily on God to prepare the way for others to learn about the way to spiritual life.

I will preserve my loving fellowship with God and others by sharing the truths I have learned with others. The value of faith in God and maintaining a daily quiet time will be seen clearly, when I reach out to others in love. Everywhere I look, there are people who need help, and I cannot always expect someone else to do the work.

My success in carrying the message will depend upon my receiving more love for the Lord Jesus and more love for others. The prayer steps to serenity are far greater than the personal peace they give me, for they insist on my speaking to others and speaking to God for others. As I surrender my life to God's everlasting love, His love in me may bring many wanderers back to Him and give them healing. Someone reached out to me and led me to faith in God. May I reach out to others so they will be able to overcome their weaknesses and find the serenity they seek.

*Today's Date:*_____

Today's Requests:

Answers to Prayer and Thanksgivings:

Daily Quiet Time Edition

About the Author

L. G. Parkhurst, Jr. is the author of *How God Teaches Us to Pray: Lessons from the Lives of Francis and Edith Schaeffer*, Word, UK, *Francis Schaeffer: the Man and His Message*, Tyndale House Publishers, and *Francis and Edith Schaeffer*, Bethany House Publishers.

He has compiled numerous devotional and prayer book classics. These books include *How to Pray in the Spirit* from the writings of John Bunyan, Kregel Publications. *Answers to Prayer* and *Principles of Prayer* from the writings of Charles G. Finney, Bethany House Publishers. *The Believer's Secret of the Abiding Presence* from the writings of Andrew Murray and Brother Lawrence, Bethany House Publishers, and *The Believer's Secret of Intercession* from the writings of Andrew Murray and C.H. Spurgeon, Bethany House Publishers. Since 1989, he has written the weekly "Bible Lesson" for *The Oklahoman,* Oklahoma's largest daily newspaper.

He received a Master of Divinity degree from Princeton Theological Seminary, Princeton, New Jersey, Master of Arts in Philosophy and Master of Library and Information Studies degrees from the University of Oklahoma, Norman, Oklahoma. He is pastor of the Stonegate Church (Cumberland Presbyterian), Edmond, Oklahoma. His church website is StonegateChurch.org. To learn more about *Prayer Steps to Serenity* and to receive additional free resources visit the PrayerSteps.org website, the SerenityGroups.org website, the SerenityJournal.org website, and the AgionPress.com website.

To order: *Prayer Steps to Serenity: Daily Quiet Time Edition* go to AgionPress.com or send $17.00 (includes shipping and handling) to Agion Press, P.O. Box 1052, Edmond, OK 73083-1052. To order *Prayer Steps to Serenity: The Twelve Steps Journey: New Serenity Prayer Edition* send $23.00 (includes shipping and handling) to the above address. Along with your check or money order, include your name and address for shipping. You can also order online or through your local bookstores.

www.ingramcontent.com/pod-product-compliance
Lightning Source LLC
Chambersburg PA
CBHW031254290426
44109CB00012B/581